The Modern Nations in
Historical Perspective

ROBIN W. WINKS, *General Editor*

The volumes in this series deal with individual nations or
groups of closely related nations throughout the world, sum-
marizing the chief historical trends and influences that have
contributed to each nation's present-day character, problems,
and behavior. Recent data are incorporated with established
historical background to achieve a fresh synthesis and original
interpretation.

TETSUO NAJITA, *an associate professor of history at the University of Chicago, is the author of* Hara Kei in the Politics of
Compromise 1905–1915. *He was awarded the John K. Fairbank Prize in East Asian History, 1969, by the American Historical Association and has written extensively on East Asian
history. He has also taught at Carleton College, Washington
University in St. Louis, and at the University of Wisconsin,
Madison.*

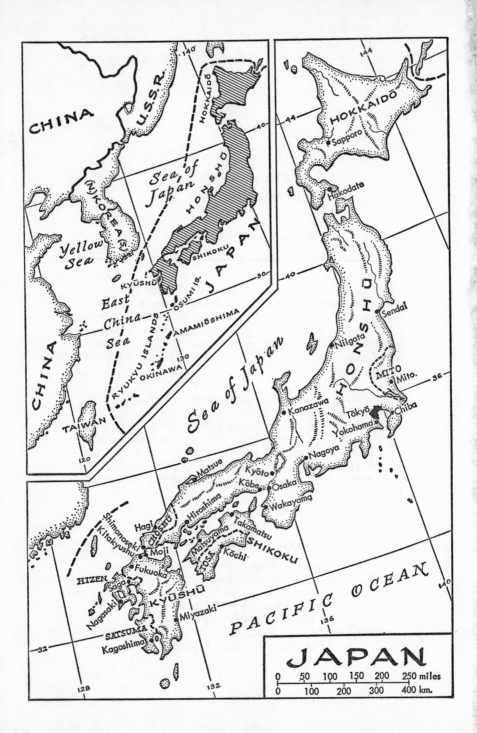

CHINA

U.S.S.R.

HOKKAIDŌ

Sea of Japan

(N) KOREA (S)

HONSHŪ

Yellow Sea

JAPAN

SHIKOKU

KYŪSHŪ

OSUMI IS.

East China Sea

RYUKYU ISLANDS

AMAMIŌSHIMA

OKINAWA

TAIWAN

HOKKAIDŌ

Sapporo

Hakodate

HONSHŪ

Sendai

Niigata

MITO
Mito.

Kanazawa

Tōkyō
Yokohama
Chiba

Sea of Japan

Nagoya

Matsue

Kyōto
Kōbe
Osaka
Wakayama

Hagi
Hiroshima
CHŌSHŪ
Shimonoseki
Kitakyushu
Moji
HIZEN
Saga
Fukuoka
Nagasaki
KYŪSHŪ
SATSUMA
Kagoshima
Miyazaki

Matsuyama
Takamatsu
SHIKOKU
TOSA
Kōchi

PACIFIC OCEAN

JAPAN

| 0 | 50 | 100 | 150 | 200 | 250 miles |

| 0 | 100 | 200 | 300 | 400 km. |

The Modern Nations in Historical Perspective

JAPAN

Tetsuo Najita

PRENTICE-HALL, INC.  Englewood Cliffs, New Jersey

A SPECTRUM BOOK

Library of Congress Cataloging in Publication Data

NAJITA, TETSUO.
   Japan.

   (Modern nations in historical perspective)
   Includes bibliographical references.
   1. Japan—History—1868–   I. Title.
DS881.9.N29   952.03   74–3337
ISBN   0–13–509455–0
ISBN   0–13–509448–8 (pbk.)

10   9   8   7   6   5   4   3   2   1

PRENTICE-HALL INTERNATIONAL, INC. (*London*)
PRENTICE-HALL OF AUSTRALIA PTY., LTD. (*Sydney*)
PRENTICE-HALL OF CANADA, LTD. (*Toronto*)
PRENTICE-HALL OF INDIA PRIVATE LIMITED (*New Delhi*)
PRENTICE-HALL OF JAPAN, INC. (*Tokyo*)

Contents

v

To Mie and Kiyoshi

Preface

This book offers an interpretive perspective on Japan as a modern nation. It is not a short history of Japan. For the general reader, it seeks to communicate something of the complexity and seriousness with which the Japanese have reflected on their own history, their politics, and their modern experience. The materials presented are not new. They are drawn from my readings of the past several years and from a few of my own writings. As the notes will suggest, they are easily accessible in Japanese and Western monographic literature. Teachers and students of Japanese studies will undoubtedly want to add more materials or suggest alternative ones. It is hoped the book will stimulate discussion, elaboration, dispute, and revision.

As is often the case with writing a book of this kind, a good deal of time was spent thinking out loud in shaping the central theme. My wife Elinor accompanied my mental peregrinations from the outset. I owe the reality of this book to her intellectual and spiritual presence. I must confess also to having turned to my colleagues in the field and to teachers and friends in Japan. I have discussed aspects of my project at Far Eastern colloquia at the

University of Wisconsin, Madison, University of Rochester, University of Washington, Seattle, and Princeton University. In the context of a continuing seminar on Japanese intellectual history supported by the National Endowment for the Humanities, Robert Bellah, Harry Harootunian, and Irwin Scheiner commented extensively and thoughtfully on my chapters at meetings held at the University of California, Berkeley, and at the University of Chicago. In the past several years either here in the United States or in Japan, Professors Mitani Taichiro, Sato Seizaburo, Ishii Shiro and Niiyama Shiseki have given generously of their knowledge. In the summer of 1971 in Tokyo, Sakai Yukichi helped me in the early stages of planning the book, and, as in past encounters, gave me valuable instruction. And finally, I presented various aspects of this book in lectures and discussions in my courses on Japanese history at the University of Chicago. I am deeply grateful to these friends, colleagues, and students, who, needless to say, have not always agreed with my views.

In the final preparation of the manuscript, Marcia Moen, Patrick Gray, and Asako Oishi gave me generous assistance, for which I am most appreciative.

1

Introduction: A Perspective
on Modern Japan

Japan presents an ambiguous image to Western eyes. One hundred million people are visualized living on four small islands (Honshū, Kyūshū, Shikoku, and Hokkaidō) with a total land area the size of California. The islands are mineral poor. In defiance of this adverse environment, however, the Japanese have attained a level of technological and industrial proficiency that many see as a truly remarkable achievement. To others, Japan incorporates the worst features of the "advanced" nations in the West; understanding Western law and constitutional procedures yet adapting them, as in its construction of a national "corporation." This view is sometimes expressed by the outlandishly egocentric American remark, "what have we wrought?" Still others see Japan's industrial and urban development, including mass consumption, intellectual pluralism, population stability in incredibly congested conditions (some twenty-five millions living in a sixty-mile radius of Tokyo alone), as evidences of a propulsion into postmodernity. And finally there are those who find that as Japan increasingly appears to resemble the West, it becomes less comprehensible; its idiosyncrasies stemming from something vaguely "feudal" or "tradi-

1

tional" that still pervades the psychology of the nation. Thus, we are reminded of the scattered pockets of lotus and chrysanthemum, aesthetic symbols of a feudal past that are immaculately preserved in an otherwise discursive sea of steel and electronics.

Behind this ambiguous image is a complex and elusive modern reality that needs to be penetrated before it can be comprehended. In this attempt, two themes will be emphasized that constitute, for the political historian, an elemental axis that is basic to an understanding of modern Japan. One of these is the pervasiveness of bureaucratic efficiency that stems from a tradition of "bureaucratism" (*kanryōshugi*). In this tradition, effective, measurable, bureaucratic performance is viewed as central to the realization of national well-being. The opposing theme, although perhaps less visible and certainly more elusive, denies the primacy of bureaucratic norms. It affirms an old and deeply felt value placed on the purity of human spirit (*ningensei; kokoro*), or the idealistic capacity in men to create and serve without regard to the self. A more modern concept of this addresses itself to the primacy of democratic value as a spiritual and cultural norm towards which society should aspire. A history of political criticism stems from an idealistic resistance against the principles of bureaucratism in modern Japan.

The importance of bureaucratism in modern Japan, of course, is beyond dispute. It undergirds the emergence of Japan as a powerful industrial nation. Certainly few will deny the amazing industrial transformation of Japan in the mid-twentieth century, following the devastating defeat in World War II, known as the Pacific War. Historians are agreed that this economic performance is neither accidental nor a mere transference of American capital and skills; and that its roots are planted deeply in indigenous soil prior to the onset of the modern century. It is part and parcel of an accumulated tradition of bureaucratic organization and of sophisticated reflections about, and attitudes toward, efficient action within structures.

The vitality of this tradition, unfortunately, is sometimes obscured. The outward features of Japan's industrial system appear new. They seem more streamlined and powerful than anything the Japanese had before the Pacific War, and certain shifts in emphasis in industrial production, as from textile to technologically complex items, have contributed to this image. More important, the constitutional guidelines are now "democratic" in contrast to those applied before the war, a particular point often used to attribute, quite deceptively, Japan's industrial recovery simply as a by-product of the American Occupation.

The Occupation did not provide Japan with a radically new leadership or program for industrial recovery. Its initial concern was to see that the Japanese people were democratic and peaceful. Thus it emphasized such measures as land reform, antitrust legislation, and the decentralization of education and the police. Large industrial facilities that escaped bombing (only about 25 percent of the total) were scheduled for dismantlement, and aid from the United States (some $2 billion over five years) came primarily in the form of surplus foodstuffs and not as capital for industrial recovery. The Occupation's vision for Japan's future was a democratic, peaceful, and basically agrarian society, a vision best captured in the now famous Article IX of the new constitution (known in Japan as the MacArthur constitution) in which the Japanese pledge as their sovereign right never to maintain "land, sea, and air forces, as well as other war potential."

The Cold War, however, forced the Occupation to revise its idealistic position. It then relied heavily on the bureaucratic and industrial leadership of the Japanese themselves; and the model of industrialization and the bureaucratic ideology first formulated and applied in the 1880s, during Japan's first industrial revolution, experienced a powerful resurgence. In the hands of Japanese leadership, the early reforms of the Occupation were revised, discarded, or ignored. The policy of dismantling Japanese industry was quietly scuttled, and antitrust legislation slowly gathered dust. The educational system was again centralized, as was the police force. Strikes and activities of the Left were suppressed as disruptive to economic recovery. High-level bureaucrats who had been purged shortly after the war ended were reinstated into government service. A military force was established because, as admitted by MacArthur himself, every nation possessed the right to defend itself.

In the 1950s this leadership converged into a powerful "establishment." [1] It is presently ensconced in key institutions such as the Economic Planning Agency, the Ministry of Finance, the Ministry of Trade and Industry, the Bank of Japan, and the Federation of Industrial Organizations (Keidanren), which sends representatives from industry to work out long-term planning with the government. Politically, the leadership is integrated into a coalition called the Liberal Democratic Party, formed in 1955 when the two prewar conservative parties joined forces. Maintaining a continuous majority in the Diet, and in turn controlling the cabinet, this party has emerged as a formidable organization, one thoroughly familiar with the strategic manipulation of political patronage and pork barrel.

But it is its agreement on policy and a shared ideology of industrialization that has made this leadership unusually strong and tenacious. There is firm agreement from the outset that capital will be generated within the country through savings and not borrowed from abroad. Capital saved will be used for capital growth, with concentrated allocation for carefully selected economic targets, and not for equitable sharing in the country. An improved economic well-being for all is promised, but, clearly, certain sectors of the economy are explicitly favored. The income tax schedule is unprogressive; profits from international trade are tax deductible; consumption taxes are imposed on items such as sake and sugar as well as on electronic equipment and appliances; direct wages are kept relatively low and benefits are extended in indirect ways, such as in bonuses, subsidies for housing, commuting, and health insurances—all devices to induce capital investment and to regulate the level of domestic consumption. Under the rubric of "industrial rationalization" (sangyō gōrika), factory units at or above a

[1] Two recent books are Nathaniel B. Thayer, *How the Conservatives Rule Japan* (New York: Columbia University Press, 1969); and Haruhiro Fukui, *Party in Power* (Berkeley: University of California Press, 1970).

certain level of productive capacity are favored through a loan policy underwritten by the Bank of Japan and other large multiregional banks. Finally, and as important a measure as not borrowing capital from abroad, the country's leaders maintain that Japan should feed itself to minimize the spending of foreign reserves on food imports. To achieve this end, the entire annual yield of rice harvest is purchased at a guaranteed price level, thus stimulating rice production (which has been maintained at surplus levels in recent years) and maximizing the efficiency of the trade structure. These various components of Japan's industrial recovery, including the facts and figures of economic growth, have often been recounted in Western-language presses and need not be detailed here.[2]

Behind this consistent policy, however, is an underlying ideological consensus, which I referred to earlier as "bureaucratism," that does deserve attention. The consensus, at times, appears to consist more of élan and mutual respect than ideology. There is also the bond of shared experiences. Members of the establishment are graduates of the same major universities. They have weathered the stringent screening for talent imposed on everyone by the educational system and the testing program—"examination hell" as it is agonizingly referred to by Japanese students. Sharing a similar theoretical, technical, and practical training, they are acutely aware of each other's abilities, which reinforces an elitist élan. But this élan also results from a shared set of ideological assumptions.

There is an ethic of achievement, of competitive self-betterment, which is at once egalitarian and elitist. It holds that everyone should have an equal opportunity (which is provided for to a significant extent through education), but that only the very best will succeed. To the successful will be entrusted the leadership of higher education, government, and industry, or, in short, the task of maintaining national well-being and dignity. This sense of responsibility for the wider society is often characterized as a remnant of "feudal paternalism," which it may well be. The psychol-

2 See Kozo Yamamura, *Economic Policy on Postwar Japan* (Berkeley: University of California Press, 1967).

ogy behind it, however, is quite complex, and it might better be thought of as a bureaucratic vision of the nation's future, for there is enormous self-confidence that, despite short-term setbacks, the bureaucracy will survive as the crucial bedrock of the nation. The primacy of rational bureaucratic management is confirmed as central to Japan's historical development and this assumption is projected into the future as a core political reality. Thus, the bureaucratic and managerial legacy of the Meiji Restoration of 1868 is glorified but not the personal and charismatic "benevolence" that one finds in a feudal past. What is emphasized is the maintenance of national integrity through collective bureaucratic expertise.

A materialistic view of society and of national independence is clearly operative in Japanese bureaucratism. It is an unadorned yet persuasive perception, having deep historical roots in traditional Japan, that maintains the nation assures its autonomy only through economic power—*fukoku*. Although shorn of the shrill rhetoric of the prewar era, this economic bureaucratism remains an unchallenged conviction of the ruling class. Bureaucratic service in Japan, then, is not simply a prestigious career or an avenue to accrue vast sums of personal wealth: it is a "mission" (*shimei*) to enhance the well-being of the nation through the systematic creation of industrial wealth.

One of the fascinating features of Japanese society today, however, is that despite a dedication to this bureaucratic mission and a general acceptance of its importance, there is also a strong and continuous countervailing attitude towards it. Bureaucratism, it is believed, is not an ideology that concerns itself with the spiritual and intellectual, or nutritive need of the nation as a whole, but is primarily an affair among the elites to satisfy their own interests. Much of society retains an ethical distance from the framework of bureaucratism, and there is considerable ambivalence toward the leadership of industry and government. Although it is generally conceded that economic rehabilitation is unthinkable without that leadership, there is conspicuous lack of emotional loyalty toward it.

Added to this wariness of bureaucratism is a traditional idealism that believes the spirit of human personality is fundamentally pure and true. It is this ideal self, or "cultural spirit," that affirms the deep value the Japanese place on humaneness (*ningensei*), that persuades men to create and act critically on behalf of others. The language of this idealism originates in the feudal past, and will be discussed as an essential component to a mode of radical protest called "restorationism."

Prior to the Pacific War, the imperial institution played a key role in this ethic. As the ultimate source of *de jure* power, it sanctioned the industrial revolution, but as a symbol of Japan's continuous cultural history it stood also for the principle of pure and selfless commitment to the national community. Above all, as god-king the emperor stood for a cultural ideal that confirmed a capacity in ordinary men to transform themselves into something extraordinary, to fully realize the dynamic and creative potential embedded in the self. The identification with this ideal sometimes led to decisive action against the present, justifying such action with the imagery and rhetoric of imperial justice for all of society. Needless to say, the integrative potential of the emperor suffered irrevocable damage in the war. Compelled by historical circumstance to shoulder the grief of the entire nation in defeat, the emperor subsequently denied publicly his sovereign character.

Although cultural idealism has lost most of its radical character of the prewar era, it survives on the current scene. In ordinary social intercourse, it is best seen in the much-discussed relationship of *giri*. In its idealistic sense, *giri* is a humane feeling of obligation one feels or ought to feel in response to a pure "blessing" (*on*) bestowed on him by another person. This reciprocation is understood as being pure and without selfish intent, as springing from one's spiritual self. Actually, it is assumed that a person rarely concedes or surrenders everything of himself. Thus, a kind act invites a reciprocal or *quid pro quo* recognition of a legitimate residuum of self-interest in the actor himself although the relationship may be uneven. Still it is clear that the primary ethical legitimation in *giri* relations is drawn directly from traditional idealistic ideas about true and humane feelings.

There is, however, a current feeling that Japanese idealism, however defined, is being directly threatened by the expansion of bureaucratism. In a recent poll an overwhelming number agreed that industrial rehabilitation was the most important achievement of the postwar era, transforming the nation from the brink of starvation in the late 1940s into a prosperous nation. About as many felt that "freedom" (*jiyū*) was also a notable achievement; and, consistent with this view, they accepted the redefined status of the emperor. Yet, most did not believe that they were happier, spiritually, in 1970, despite prosperity and democracy, than their predecessors before the war. Many felt that the single most important "loss" of the postwar era has been "human spirit" (*kokoro*); and they wished future achievements would restore "humaneness" or a feeling of "humanity" (*ningensei*) in Japanese society.[3]

The regret expressed may not simply mean a longing for an idyllic past, but a desire to achieve something new and contrastive to those values identified with past disasters. Nevertheless, attitudes expressed in the poll just cited underscore an important characteristic of the Japanese perception of themselves. While not seeking to revive prewar emperorism, the Japanese remain very much an emotional and spiritual people. As reindustrialization becomes an accomplished fact, there is increasing introspection about deeper spiritual needs, which all agree bureaucratism cannot provide.

In recent years, for example, there has been a renewed interest in history. The meaning of tradition is once again being discussed with far less opprobrium than in the immediate postwar years. Books abound dealing with the elemental cultural values of *giri*, beauty, religious beliefs, and community relations. Historical novels of the medieval period are extremely popular, and some of them have been brilliantly serialized on television. A best seller has recounted the origins of the Pacific War within a broad historical framework describing it as "the first one hundred years'

[3] The poll is published in *Mainichi shimbun*, August 15, 1970.

war in Asia." And the novelist Mishima Yukio warned his readers of the deterioration of the Japanese "people," due to the excessive concern with economic growth, into an indistinguishable "crowd" devoid of a distinctive culture and a creative ethos.[4]

Despite the previous discussion, it would be erroneous to see the distrust of bureaucratism as merely a revival of traditional idealism. The immediate postwar years witnessed an articulate mass movement for a new democracy that set out to fulfill the work begun in the "Enlightenment" of the 1870s and the struggle for popular government in the 1920s. Conscious of previous failures in history, the movement turned its iconoclasm against "authoritarianism," "feudalism," and "fascism"—all the attitudes and concepts that had previously prevented Japan from realizing true modernity. With unusual vigor and eloquence, as in the writings of Maruyama Masao,[5] it was argued that what could not be achieved in the past could now be realized since there was popular sovereignty, universal suffrage, civil liberties, and a constitution outlawing war. Unobstructed by the institutional constraints of the past, the nation could move toward the democratization of the Japanese spirit. A rarity in modern Japanese intellectual history, much of the nation, prewar and postwar generations alike, including the militant Left, moderate socialists, and progressive liberals, shared in the iconoclastic esprit and the optimism of the movement for democracy following the end of the war.

The optimism was to be short-lived. Despite the democratic constitution, the structure of power within it appeared to have more of the markings of prewar politics than of the new democ-

----

[4] Mishima's views are clearly expressed in Mishima Yukio and Hayashi Fusao, *Taiwa: Nihonjinron* (Tokyo: Banchō shobō, 1966). Also of interest is Hayashi Fusao, *Daitōa sensō kōteiron*, 2 vols. (Tokyo: Banchō shobō, 1964–65). Essays dealing with *giri* and the Japanese psychology are Minamoto Ryōen, *Giri to ninjō* (Tokyo: Chūōkōronsha, 1969); and Minami Hiroshi, *Nihonjin no shinri* (Tokyo: Iwanami shoten, 1953), which has gone through at least twenty-three printings.

[5] Some of Maruyama's essays have been translated into English in Ivan Morris, ed., *Thought and Behavior in Modern Japan* (London: Oxford University Press, 1963).

racy envisioned after the defeat. All through the 1950s it became increasingly clear that the democratic constitution could be made to reinforce the policies of reindustrialization in ways that were frankly undemocratic, and that the postwar bureaucratic and industrial elites could operate quite effectively and comfortably within that order and continue to direct public participation in the processes of economic expansion. Moreover, the consolidation of the conservative coalition against the socialist movement predicted a political scheme in which the Liberal Democratic Party would control the Diet and the election process. This party has in fact dominated national politics down to the present, maintaining a "permanent" majority in the Diet and relegating the socialists to a continuing minority status.[6]

Despite these powerful trends, the value of democracy remains important to contemporary Japan. An abstract normative value of rational humanitarianism, it acts as a point of reference outside of existing politics and history. In this respect, democracy is a radical concept in Japan, not a pragmatic one about the political process. It provides an ethical identification with which to criticize historical trends and the cultural and political content of the present. As in the 1920s before the war, democracy is not an empowering ideology for constitutional politics, but critical and quite often antipolitical.

As the obvious gap between ethical expectation and structured political process widened in the 1950s, the movement for democracy inevitably found itself severely divided over the proper strategy for protest. University students, in particular, urged militant confrontation with the forces of bureaucratic government. A great many turned away from the proponents of moderation and peaceful protest—the "progressives"—and actively supported the Japanese Communist party, only to be rebuked by the Cominform in 1955 for adventurism. The details of Stalinism that came to be known in these years further stunned the militant Left. Idealistic

---

[6] This situation appears to have changed somewhat in the past year or two. The socialist party has captured the mayorships of Tokyo, Osaka, Kyoto, indicating a growing strength in urban centers.

liberals and progressives, on the other hand, were deeply disillusioned by the reversals in Occupation policies and in particular Japan's forced signature of a bilateral mutual security pact in 1951 with the United States instead of a multilateral peace settlement that included China and Soviet Russia.

The impact of these events has been lasting, and there has yet to emerge a commanding consensus on the matter of protest strategy. Although not readily visible to the Western eye, the disillusionment has been deep among the politically articulate strata.[7] There remains, however, a continuing belief in the need to protest and resist the flow of history as it is being channeled by bureaucratism. There continues a high-mindedness and intelligence in these voices of protest, and there can be little doubt but that they shall persist as a continuing reminder of higher humanitarian goals toward which society should aim.

Traditional idealism and the more modern conception of democratic value are certainly not of the same order of things, a point that need not be labored. But it is important to observe that both are essentially nonbureaucratic, and potentially antibureaucratic, modes of thought. Both emphasize the ethical and spiritual dimension of social existence. Above all, both themes are inextricably woven into a long history of criticism and protest against bureaucratic government that spans the entire course of Japan's modern history.

It is premature at this juncture to say what sort of balance between bureaucratism and idealism will be realized in the future. At present, however, it is clear that the forces of bureaucratism have been preponderant. In quality, unlike any other previous phase in the postwar era, therefore, the Japanese are extremely sensitive to the uncertainties created by the reindustrialization of the country. They feel in full force the contradictory currents alluded to in this introduction. There is pervasive bureaucratism, which includes a belief in the primacy of economic forces for personal and national advancement. Virtually everyone accepts

[7] This critical disillusionment is reflected, for example, in Maruyama Masao, *Nihon no shisō* (Tokyo: Iwanami shoten, 1961).

Japan's industrial revolutions (in the 1880s and 1950s) as irreversible historical events. Hardly anyone speaks of returning to agrarian seclusionism as a viable option. There is, however, psychological and intellectual disquiet, a feeling of ambivalence and anticlimax.

A sober mood prevails that an era is ending, what might be called a feeling of "Late Showa" (Shōwa makki), an introspectiveness accompanynig the end of a reign period that resembles the fin de siècle in Western societies. Reminiscent of "Late Meiji," the decade or so following the victory in the Russo-Japanese War in 1905, the Japanese have turned their "achievement" into historical introspection and raised questions about themselves and the purpose and quality of their future. These questions have refocused attention on fundamental cultural values, of the belief in human feeling, and about the possibility and significance of continuous protest and criticism in the light of expanding bureaucratic power. Despite differences in the descriptive language and metaphor, this is a theme that is woven into Japan's modern history and remains a central historical perspective on Japan as a modern society.

In the pages that follow, I shall attempt to develop the interpretive perspective sketched out in this introduction through an examination of the past. A number of different points in time might be selected to enter into a discussion of Japanese history. There is an ancient beginning, according to nationalistic mythology before the war, 660 B.C. All events within a continuous history, it was argued, are logically interconnected so that Japan's history should be retraced from the beginning, prior to the Sino-Buddhist impacts of the sixth and seventh centuries A.D. and developed into modern times.

A view of the entire sweep of known history provides several other more crucial dates for turning points where the historian might begin his narrative. In 645 A.D. Japan deliberately set out, in what is called the Taika Reform, to establish a centralized monarchical system patterned on the T'ang codes of China. The underlying intent behind this effort was the incorporation of a rational principle of hierarchy, and hence of authority, to provide order in a situation of endemic strife among rival clan groupings. In 1185, following several centuries of deteriorating efforts at centralized bureaucratic rule, a distinctive form of government called *bakufu*, or government under a military hegemon, the *shōgun*, was established at Kamakura. The purpose here was a systematic form of rule to regularize landed and military concentrations of power that had grown up outside of the legal bureaucracy. A third major point in Japan's history is 1600, which begins the rule of the Tokugawa *bakufu*, the third and most effective of *bakufu* governments, and named after its founder Tokugawa Ieyasu (1542–1616). One among several powerful contending barons, or *daimyō*, seeking national unification, Tokugawa Ieyasu emerged victorious to dictate a decisive political settlement. It was during this Tokugawa era that a stable pattern of bureaucratic rule was established, decisively influencing the political character of modern Japan. The Tokugawa era ended in 1868 with the Meiji Restoration, which was Japan's modern revolution. One final important date is 1945, the well-known end of the disastrous Pacific War and the beginning of the dramatic postwar industrial recovery. Each of these dates stands for a culmination of a complex history and each left in its wake a powerful and multifaceted legacy. Students of history may wish for an account that somehow seeks to connect all of these key turning points into a coherent evolutionary scheme, but I have not relied on such an approach in this short study on modern Japan. In an interpretive analysis, the historian is required to limit his thematic focus and chronological coverage.

An understanding of Japan as a modern nation through a study of the past requires that we see in the main what Japanese bureaucratism was like as it appeared in its most mature and stable form prior to the modern revolution in the mid-nineteenth century. This book, therefore, will enter into Japanese history at the turning point of 1600, for it is in the Tokugawa period that a bureaucratic order was established upon which much of modern Japan rests, not so much in static structures as in attitudes, modes of perception, and patterns of action. It is in this period that Japan may be thought of as having become "political" for the first time in the sense of perceiving itself conceptually as a structured bureaucratic society and developing a political language for discourse on the theory and ethical significance of bureaucratic action. There were undoubtedly powerful antecedent historical forces at work that helped shape such a society, a point that is beyond dispute; but I wish to emphasize in this account the view of Tokugawa society as the culmination or high point of Japan as a traditional society from which the historian might extract those legacies that seem to reach in complex ways into making Japan a modern nation. In particular, I shall underscore a deep and elemental political current, which I have called "restorationism," that flows through the Tokugawa period and spills over into the modern era. The political consciousness that accompanied this powerful flow goes far toward explaining why this "late feudal" experience in Tokugawa Japan should justly be understood as a distinctive experience in Far Eastern history. Modern Japan is unthinkable without this background.

The chapters that follow, then, present the outlines of an interpretive construct, an organizing thought about modern Japanese history, and are not intended to be a comprehensive narrative. Accordingly, the following chapter discusses Tokugawa bureaucratic structure and key formulations of bureaucratic ideology. The discussion defines the tension between bureaucratic politics and articulate attempts to explain the scope and practical limits of bureaucracy. In chapter 3, idealistic action theories are presented as ethical criticism of bureaucracy and of bureaucratic loyalism. In conjunction with pragmatic thought about bureaucracy, this idealistic theme is central to restorationism, the conceptual framework within which the feudal order was destroyed beginning with the Meiji Restoration of 1868. The reformulation of bureaucratic politics into a constitutional structure during the Meiji period (1868–1912) is then discussed (chapter 4) and related to new intellectual attempts to revalidate loyal bureaucratic and idealistic action in the context of pervasive historical change. This is followed by a discussion in chapters 5 and 6 of the legacy of the Meiji Restoration in the development of political change and of protest in early twentieth-century Japan before the Pacific War. Emphasis is placed on the redefinition of constitutional politics and ideology as well as the growth of voices of discontent among nationalists, liberals, socialists, and, in particular, radical restorationists in the 1930s.

The overall view presented here is that the history of modern Japan is not a unilinear achievement of higher levels of rationality, an image often conveyed or expected of modern Japan, but that on the contrary it is a history full of dispute and intellectual tension. It is a view that hopefully will sensitize us to some of the questions being raised today in Japan about what lies beyond bureaucratic achievement for the future of Japanese culture.

2

The Tokugawa
Bureaucratic Legacy

The development of a political tradition in Japan is exceedingly complex. It is a tradition that predates the coming of "civilization," that is, the Sino-Buddhist cultural impact of the sixth and seventh centuries, and continues through the "medieval" periods between the ninth and sixteenth centuries. Throughout the Fujiwara, Kamakura and Ashikaga periods,[1] tortuous attempts were made, with varying degrees of effectiveness, to construct a stable bureaucratic system. Yet it was not until the Tokugawa

[1] These are the three main political periods falling between the Taika Reform of 645 and the founding of the Tokugawa *bakufu* in 1600. The dates usually given for these periods are: Fujiwara, 857–1160; Kamakura, 1185–1333; and Ashikaga, 1336–1573. Good general coverage of these periods are Peter Duus, *Feudalism in Japan* (New York: Alfred A. Knopf, 1969); Edwin O. Reischauer, *Japan: The Story of a Nation* (New York: Alfred A. Knopf, 1970; first published in 1946 as *Japan Past and Present*); John K. Fairbank, Edwin O. Reischauer, and Albert M. Craig, *East Asia: Tradition and Transformation* (Boston: Houghton Mifflin Company, 1973); John W. Hall, *Japan from Prehistory to Modern Times* (New York: Delacorte Press, 1970; first published in Germany in 1968 as *Das Japanische Kaiserreich*). The outstanding monograph is John W. Hall, *Government and Local Power in Japan 500 to 1700* (Princeton: Princeton University Press, 1966).

period (1600–1868), in what is sometimes referred to as "early modern" or "late traditional" Japan, that such a structure was forged. Equally as important, politics became articulate and critical in a quality and degree that was unprecedented in Japanese history. As political structure and as thought, the foundations of modern Japan can best be seen in the Tokugawa bureaucratic order.

During its two hundred fifty years of seclusion, relative domestic peace, and extraordinary cultural expression in the *haiku*, *kabuki*, and woodblock prints, the Tokugawa period witnessed a regulated, efficient, and predictable bureaucratic performance that became a conscious and articulate part of Japanese politics. From a mandate to maintain "Peace and Tranquility Throughout the Land" (*Tenka taihei*), bureaucratic activity steadily gained wider significance to include providing security and economic well-being for the entire polity. The concept of polity itself gained wider bureaucratic significance, initially indicating semiautonomous territorial domains, *han* or *kuni*, and growing to mean a single comprehensive administrative entity, or nation, which was also referred to as *kuni*.

There emerged in this period a tradition of political discourse about the nature of bureaucracy, the legitimacy of pragmatic action within fixed structures, and the limits of bureaucratic perception and action. There originated conceptual attempts to justify bureaucratic structures, and therefore of action within them, as historically valid, ethically defensible, and potentially lasting into the future. This might be thought of as the conscious formulation of political "ideology." In contrast, though perhaps less visible and less conspicuous in most historical accounts, there was the skeptical denial of bureaucratic "reason" as an adequate ethic of action. In this alternative tradition, there was a quest for an autonomous idealistic basis for action, which, toward the latter part of the era especially, was expressed in harsh criticism of some of the prevailing justifications of bureaucratic action. The historical roots of Japan's radical nationalist tradition are to be found in this political idealism.

The Tokugawa political legacy, then, is a complicated one and crucial for an understanding of modern Japan. It suggests a highly sophisticated political society, "traditional" yet expressive of a wide range of key problems of politics in history. In the following discussion, a brief characterization of the Tokugawa bureaucratic system, the *baku-han* order, will be followed by an analysis of "ideology," especially as it points to bureaucratic action. The idealistic critique of bureaucratism will be discussed in the following chapter on "restorationism."

THE BAKU-HAN BUREAUCRATIC STRUCTURE

The Tokugawa bureaucratic system was a decentralized or semicentralized form of governance. Observers even then were struck by its seemingly odd and contrived features, especially when contrasted to the brilliantly symmetrical Chinese model of imperial rule or the monarchical absolutism of some European nations. Yet there was political intelligence and intent behind the peculiar design. It was a bureaucratic settlement to incorporate and reconcile conflicting identifications with land, military power, and the ethic of loyalty. Throughout Japan's medieval history (ca. 1100–1600), these irreconcilable identifications resulted in the repeated sacrificing of wider ties of loyalty for closer, strategically more relevant, considerations of land and security. Endemic warfare was common through much of this period. Following the decisive military victory at the battle of Sekigahara in 1600, the Tokugawa house, headed by Tokugawa Ieyasu, framed a settlement that would regenerate the principle of wider loyalties and avoid a reversion to the use of "loyalty" as justification for conflict between contending baronial alignments. Yet, in working out this settlement, total centralization, the widest extension of loyalty that is politically conceivable, was considered impractical and rejected.

Tokugawa Ieyasu was well aware that "loyalty" does not necessarily blend itself with "power" into a single undifferentiated unit. "Loyalty" (*chū*), he reasoned with his adviser Fujiwara

Seika (1561–1619), might be a theoretical absolute, a metaphysical *princip* as described in Sung Neo-Confucian ethical thought, but it was not identical with "power" (*ken*), which had a historical reality of its own. Politics was the working out of the relationship between the two spheres: The issue was not whether "power" could be transformed totally into a principle of loyalty or to become one with the "way," but whether ethical principle could be accommodated and incorporated into existing power relationships. It was unquestionably this latter perception of "loyalty" and "power" that governed the Tokugawa settlement.[2]

Total centralization might invite protracted civil war by *daimyō* with powerful regional bases to defend. It followed that the principle of loyalty should not be applied exclusively for centralization but used also to allow, within prescribed limits, a regional structure of loyal relations. Thus, despite the undeniable hegemony of the Tokugawa *bakufu* ensconced in Edo, the system was curiously decentralized. Key political balances were struck to allow for regional autonomy.

As discussed by Conrad Totman in his excellent study of Tokugawa politics,[3] the *bakufu* assured military and economic preponderance for itself, directly controlling one-fourth of the rice yield in the country and retaining the unilateral prerogative to use military force against transgressors of its laws. Especially stringent were laws forbidding lateral baronial alliances. The *bakufu*, however, pledged not to use force if its rules were respected, a pledge that it abided by with unusual consistency once order was assured in the mid-seventeenth century. It also allowed *daimyō* to remain as lords of *han* domains, of which there were about two hundred fifty of varying types and shapes, and within which the *daimyō*

[2] Bitō Masahide discusses this in "Hōken rinri," *Iwanami kōza, Nihon rekishi*, vol. 10, *Kinsei*, 2 (Tokyo: Iwanami shoten, 1963), pp. 273–312, esp. 281–93.

[3] Conrad Totman, *Politics in the Tokugawa Bakufu* (Cambridge: Harvard University Press, 1967). Useful essays are found in John W. Hall and Marius B. Jansen, eds., *Studies in the Institutional History of Early Modern Japan* (Princeton: Princeton University Press, 1968). A series of essays by leading Japanese scholars is collected in *Iwanami kōza, Nihon rekishi*, vol. 10.

retained administrative authority in judicial, fiscal, agricultural, and educational matters. A most unusual concession allowed individual *daimyō* to retain a separate vassalage, *samurai* who owed direct loyalty to them as lords of *han*, and not to the *shōgun* as head of the *bakufu*.

Within this framework of agreement, the *bakufu* worked out arrangements between itself and various groups of *daimyō*, apportioning "land," "military function," and "bureaucratic responsibility." To three collateral houses (*shimpan*) established to assure continuity in the shogunal line, the *bakufu* granted large wealthy domains and the important military function of guarding the main marches into the Kantō plain where the *bakufu* was situated; but it did not concede to these prestigious blood relations political or administrative responsibility in the actual operation of the *bakufu*'s government in Edo. To some of its trusted vassals (called *fudai*, and not related by blood to the Tokugawa house), the *bakufu* assigned small- and medium-sized domains without significant military responsibilities attached to them; but entrusted to these *fudai* vassals the primary responsibility of actually operating the *bakufu* bureaucracy. A large portion of the income of these vassal bureaucrats came from stipends from bureaucratic service, not from the produce of their domains.

Other direct vassals, also called *fudai*, were given large strategic domains in the regions with security responsibilities but were denied a bureaucratic role in Edo. "Bannermen" (*hatamoto*) and "housemen" (*gokenin*), vassals below the *fudai* stratum, were concentrated in Edo, entrusted with important defense and police functions that gave them stipends and prestige; but they were not allowed into the upper reaches of the bureaucracy nor were they allotted large- or even medium-sized domains.

Finally, there were baronial "allies" called "outer lords," or *tozama*. To those allies who had sided with Ieyasu in his march to power, the *bakufu* granted large domains and strategic security functions but no bureaucratic responsibilities in the operation of the *bakufu* bureaucracy. To those allies who swore loyalty *after* being defeated at the military denouement at Sekigahara in 1600 (the most famous examples are Satsuma and Chōshū in western Japan), the *bakufu* reduced their domains in size and denied them both military responsibilities in the regions and bureaucratic duties in Edo; but like other *daimyō*, they retained control over a separate vassalage and the internal administration of their domains.

This seemingly mechanical distribution of power and wealth was accompanied by a drastic redefinition of previous political and social history. Each domain could have only one castle town, all other strategic bastions had to be dismantled. *Daimyō* had to visit Edo periodically and leave behind hostages (a system called *sankin kōtai*), forcing them to build several sumptuous mansions for these hostages and for a sizable service retinue. *Daimyō* that appeared recalcitrant or potentially troublesome were stripped of power and status. Most drastic of all, members of the entire *samurai* class were forced to choose either to live in a single castle town where the *daimyō* resided and serve as stipended bureaucrats or on the land and surrender their aristocratic status. Severing the aristocracy from land, certainly one of the most distinctive features of Tokugawa political history, was entirely consistent with the *bakufu's* calculated creation of a separate, regionally based, structure of loyalty. Thus, although *samurai* in the various *han* would owe loyalty to their *daimyō* and not directly to the Edo *bakufu*, they would be forbidden to receive grants of land and to live on and administer these as part of their aristocratic responsibilities. Such redistribution of land would surely have led to a centrifugal process beyond *bakufu* control, and it was carefully circumscribed through legal fiat.

After offering the *samurai* a "choice" of living on the land or in castle towns, the *bakufu* proceeded to limit the size of that class. The rapid mobility into this class during a century and more of warfare struck the *bakufu* as being a source of political and economic insecurity, and it proscribed further circulation into it. This decree was consistently enforced by the *bakufu*, in contrast to its actions regarding movement between the other major functional classes of the farmers, artisans, and merchants.

This calculated use of aristocratic social organization had two historical precedents. Prior to the Sino-Buddhist impact of the seventh century, aristocracy was defined according to membership in kinship and functional groupings (*uji*), which presumably traced themselves to distant ancestral deities. With the Taika Reform of 645 A.D., aristocracy was redefined to accord with legally defined positions in a bureaucratic hierarchy (patterned after the T'ang system). Thus, while much of the social content of aristocracy remained the same, the definitional underpinnings were drastically rationalized.

In more ad hoc fashion, another pervasive repatterning of aristocracy took place in the eleventh and twelfth centuries. Identification with bureaucratic status steadily deteriorated in significance and was gradually replaced by ties of mutual loyalty between a servitor, or *samurai*, and a regional baron, or *daimyō*. The actual social content of aristocracy, however, continued to fluctuate violently all through the fifteenth and sixteenth centuries. The ideal of a "high" aristocracy buttressed by pedigree, culture, and tradition could not be maintained while men of humble social origins, some directly from the soil itself (called appropriately *jizamurai*), made their way as "loyal" fighting men into the *samurai* "aristocracy." Indeed, the three main figures responsible for Japan's reunification in the late sixteenth century, Oda Nobunaga (1534–82), Toyotomi Hideyoshi (1536–98), and Tokugawa Ieyasu himself all had dubious genealogies.

In the Tokugawa revision the tradition of aristocracy was preserved. But the *bakufu* defined that aristocracy in a manner that departed significantly from the past. The *samurai* aristocrat was not so much a loyal fighting man with landed interests to defend, but a bureaucrat serving in cities, living apart from the land, and receiving a stipend for his service. Presented with the option of land or status, most *samurai* chose bureaucratic status and city life. In 1850 between 6 and 8 percent of the total population of about 30 million were *samurai*, and they remained disproportionately large among traditional aristocracies. Of greater importance, these *samurai* were an urban-based aristocracy: 50 percent of the population of castle towns, which ranged in size from 10,000 to 200,000 were *samurai* or families of *samurai*. The same proportion held true of Edo, which had grown from a fishing village of about 10,000 in the beginning of the Tokugawa period into a metropolis of over 1 million inside of a century.

The Tokugawa transformation of the aristocratic tradition in this regard is fundamental to modern Japanese history. Within the oddly designed "feudal" order, the *samurai* were substantially reoriented in the course of the Tokugawa period into an urban bureaucratic elite.

Disconnected from land, fully literate, armed with special bureaucratic skills in fiscal, educational, and agricultural matters (for which they received a "salary"), and invested with the powerful historical symbol of the sword (which they were not expected to use), the *samurai* were an aristocracy of an unusual sort, one as conscious of its immediate calling in loyal bureaucratic service as in its heritage as a fighting aristocracy. Above all, it was an aristocracy trained to serve a particular lord and that lord's "realm," the *han*.[4]

Only the *daimyō* could possess land. On condition of loyalty to the *bakufu*, the *han* was the lord's polity. He was not allowed as a general rule to subdivide, sell, grant, or will any portion of it to kin and favorites. The *han* came to signify a fixed legal entity, indivisible, and the lord's responsibility alone to manage and maintain. It could be passed on to only one son, usually the eldest, although a younger and more talented one could be selected in certain situations.

The social principle governing this definition of the *daimyō*'s domain was that of the "house," or *ie*. According to the pioneering anthropologists on this subject, Aruga Kizaemon and Yanagida Kunio, the *ie* was grounded in ancient history.[5] It was a multi-

---

[4] See Ronald B. Dore, *Education in Tokugawa Japan* (Berkeley: University of California Press, 1965).

[5] Aruga Kizaemon, *Aruga Kizaemon chosakushū*, 10 vols. (Tokyo: Mirai-sha, 1967), especially vols. 7 and 9, dealing with the problem of the Japanese *ie* and social structure, and also vol. 4, pp. 177-352. Yanagida Kunio's discussion can be found in his *Kaheidan* (Tokyo: Kamakura shobō, 1946). A readable discussion of this subject is presented in Bitō Masahide, ed., *Chūgoku bunka sōshō*, vol. 10, *Nihon bunka to Chūgoku* (Tokyo: Taishūkan shoten, 1968), especially Bitō's introduction, pp. 1–22.

kinship functional commune whose head (called *oya* or *oyakata*) symbolized power and talent and assumed responsibility for the prosperity and continuity of the entire group. The members were called *ko*, meaning "workers." Although at some undetermined point *oya* and *ko* came to mean parent and child, they continued to retain a functional nonkinship meaning as well, which helps to explain the virtually undifferentiated character of "loyalty to lord" (*chū*) and "piety to parent" (*kō*), both of which were linked in a single compound.

The *han* was a politicized expression of this social system. The *daimyō* was the *oya* figure who symbolized talent and power and who was responsible for managing the affairs of the entire polity, assuring its prosperity and future as a unified administrative entity. *Samurai* played a crucial role by serving and thus aiding the *daimyō* to fulfill his responsibilities to the polity. In turn, *samurai* were responsible for maintaining their individual "houses," supported by stipends. Just as the *daimyō* might not divide his *han*, the individual *samurai* was not at liberty to subdivide and will his stipend. His stipend, like the *han*, could be bequeathed to only one person.

As a principle of social organization, then, the *ie* encompassed politics, blood, and economics: It perpetuated political status and territory, assured genealogical continuity and hence consistency in the social content of aristocracy, and minimized the dispersion of available wealth. While the principle was not new to the Tokugawa period, its generalized and systematic application gave to it a new significance, providing uniformity and overall internal coherence and symmetry to the structure of regional autonomy. In the *samurai*'s service to his lord and the lord's "house," the idea of *ie* remained intact, but it was reapplied to incorporate political and bureaucratic function and the meaning of polity itself. From Tokugawa times, polity steadily came to mean the accumulated wealth, talent, and strength of "houses." Indeed, the "nation" in modern Japan may be thought of as an interrelationship of functional houses (*kokka*); and the term often used in modern times to mean the "public realm" (*ōyake*) literally means "great house."

The *bakufu* accompanied the political use of the principle of *ie* with other measures, some of which were quite drastic. Although it allowed regional autonomy, the *bakufu* strictly forbade inter-*han* diplomacy. Similarly, it ordered the *daimyō* to sever all previous contacts with foreign powers. Rather than undertake the enormous task of enforcing this latter decree, the *bakufu* ordered the entire country closed, except for the port of Nagasaki, which it directly administered. Japanese traders and pirates who had marauded the Chinese and Southeast Asian coast lines in the sixteenth century were ordered to return home or become permanent exiles. Foreign commerce as a source of wealth was rejected as unnecessary for Japan's needs, despite two previous centuries of extensive trade, and agriculture received major emphasis. Military expansionism of the sort launched by Toyotomi Hideyoshi's invasion of Korea in the early 1590s was likewise rejected. Christianity was banned. In short, the *bakufu* reversed the expansive tendencies of the sixteenth century, which emphasized the need for greater centralization, and chose splendid seclusionism and the allowance of domestic baronial autonomy. Viewed from this perspective, the dogmatic insistence on the primacy of agriculture over trade, the glorification of the sword over the Western gun, and the prizing of seclusion over exposure to Christianity are to be seen less as indications of intrinsic Japanese paranoia, although some of the rhetoric of this period plays on paranoic fears, but more as interrelated guidelines of political and bureaucratic organization upon which the *baku-han* system relied for its structural integrity.

In viewing the pattern of activity and mobility within the Tokugawa bureaucratic structure several critical nexus of power stand out. There is first the *bakufu* itself, holding preponderant economic and military power and ensconced in Edo, a massive preindustrial city of comparable size to London in the eighteenth century. Second, there is a horizontal or lateral structure connecting the *bakufu* in Edo with 250 semiautonomous *han*, each with a charter stipulating the nature of the relationship. Within each of these *han* there is a vertical hierarchy to service the *han* bureaucracy in the regions as well as the lord's several mansions in

Edo. Bureaucratic activity and mobility occurred along these nexus. Prestige went to those whose responsibilities were complex and important, with upward mobility often occurring without change in one's official status or income. Competition centered on who would do what, where (it was desirable to accompany the retinue to Edo), and for how long. Although competition was constrained, it was urgent to the *samurai*, as they were bureaucrats for life, without prospect of early retirement to the land.

The stability of the system depended in large measure on the extent to which its principles of organization could be maintained. However, its reliance on seclusionism and agrarianism to permit regional autonomy led the structure to its inevitable doom. The *baku-han* system could not have survived into the twentieth century—it would have been battered from without or perhaps gutted from within. Yet, what needs to be assessed properly is not that this traditional order could not have survived the modern challenge, but that it functioned effectively for 200 years and left a profound legacy of dynamic bureaucratic performance. Above all, the transformation of the *samurai* from a warrior class to a bureaucratic elite was sufficient to trigger an intellectual process of self-reflection, research, and expression about the meaning of "bureaucratic" and "loyal" action within structures that are "fixed." The bureaucratic experience of the Tokugawa period, then, was not merely a record of mechanical and routinized performance, but a provocative and vigorous expansion in the political consciousness of the ruling class, and a good part of the rest of society as well. It was in the formulation and articulation of an "ideology" that bureaucratism became perceptive and critical, facilitating its transference as a mode of action from "feudal" structures into modern "constitutional" ones.

BUREAUCRATIC IDEOLOGY IN TOKUGAWA JAPAN

The conscious use of secular political ideas in the seventeenth and eighteenth centuries to legitimate political structures was in quality and degree without precedent in Japanese history. Impressive articulations, either in formal Chinese-style prose (*kambun*), or less formal Japanese-style prose (*kanamajiribun*), discussed the historical and theoretical underpinnings of bureaucratic structure (*seido*, as this was commonly called) and especially how loyal men ought to act in an ethically designed political system.

These ideas were drawn in the main from classical Chinese canons and scholarly commentaries. Whereas the governing intellectual force during the previous 1,000 years may be characterized as being primarily Buddhist, Japan during the Tokugawa era concentrated with sudden and conspicuous intensity on Confucian studies. This is not as perplexing as it may seem at first glance. Just as the teachings of Christ or the ideas of Plato, Machiavelli, and Marx can take on new significance in a political and social reality radically different from the original historical context, so too in Tokugawa Japan the ideas of Confucianism, which had developed over centuries in China and which had been known only to a small circle of Buddhist scholars in medieval Japan, now suddenly gained new intellectual vitality and importance. What is crucial is that these ideas were used as intellectual devices with which to reflect on what appeared to be the achievement of a stable political and social settlement and to explain it in the light of previous historical development. Used in this explanatory manner, these ideas gained a new application in Japan, imparting a rationality to the understanding of the past, a practical consciousness about political economy, and, in the course of the Tokugawa period, a provocative awareness of national distinctiveness. A proper understanding of the intellectual history of this period, then, is not that the ideas had antecedent statements in a parent culture and therefore lacked originality, but that these ideas gained creative use and expression in a divergent political context, thus playing a decisive role in the shaping of a modern society.

The leading voices were in private academies: Itō Jinsai (1627–1705) of the Horikawa School and Yamazaki Ansai (1618–82) of Kimon, both of Kyoto; Ogyū Sorai (1666–1728) of Ken'en and Dazai Shundai (1680–1747) of Shishien, both of Edo; Nakai

Shūan (1643–1758) and his sons Chikuzan (1730–1804) and Riken (1732–1817) of the Kaitokushoin in Osaka. There were also independent scholars such as Kaibara Ekken (1630–1714) and Nakae Tōju (1608–48), who commanded great respect and admiration in their day.[6] The list is extensive, and the degree of interschool and interpersonal communication and debate far exceeds what has generally been expected of Tokugawa society. Ideas discussed and formulated were published in the cities and read in *han*-sponsored schools in the regions, and the effects of this discourse on the political consciousness of modern Japan have been deep and lasting.

The ideological basis of the Tokugawa order was not a single system of thought. Having conceded regional *han* autonomy, the *bakufu* relinquished the authority to impose, as through the examination system of China, an "orthodoxy" throughout the country. Even within its area of political jurisdiction, the *bakufu* did not insist on a systematic "orthodoxy." Although it favored Neo-Confucianism and the Hayashi School, it permitted hundreds of

---

6 David Magerey Earl, *Emperor and Nation in Japan* (Seattle: University of Washington Press, 1964); Herschel Webb, *The Japanese Imperial Institution in the Tokugawa Period* (New York: Columbia University Press, 1968). Two outstanding works in Japanese are Maruyama Masao, *Nihon seiji shisōshi kenkyū* (Tokyo: Tokyo daigaku shuppankai, 1952); and Bitō Masahide, *Nihon hōken shisōshi kenkyū* (Tokyo: Aoki shoten, 1961). Bitō emphasizes Yamazaki Ansai's stream of thought and contrasts it with that of Nakae Tōju, the critic of the system. Maruyama focuses on Ogyū Sorai and his legacy. The interpretations (and style) of these two scholars are quite different. It should be observed that Bitō wrote with Maruyama's pioneering research in mind. An excellent study that takes its point of departure from Maruyama and Bitō is Tahara Tsuguo, *Tokugawa shisoshi kenkyu* (Tokyo: Miraisha, 1967); and also his "Edo jidai zenki no rekishi shisō," in *Nihon shisōshi kenkyūkai*, ed., *Nihon ni okeru rekishi shisō no tenkai* (Tokyo: Yoshikawa kōbunkan, 1965), pp. 183–212. In a more general vein is Sagara Tōru, *Kinsei no jukyō shisō* (Tokyo: Hanawa shobō, 1966); and more recently, Minamoto Ryōen, *Tokugawa gōrishisō no keifu* (Tokyo: Chūōkōronsha, 1972). The standard work of prewar scholarship, which is still invaluable, is Inoue Tetsujirō, *Nihon Yōmeigakuha no tetsugaku* (Tokyo: Fūzambō, 1900); and two sequels, *Nihon kogakuha no tetsugaku* (1902) and *Nihon Shushigakuha no tetsugaku* (1905). A student in Japanese studies interested in this area might start with Matsumoto Sannosuke's lectures, *Nihon seijishisō gairon* (Tokyo: Keisō shobō, 1964).

private schools in Edo which taught a wide range of ideas, and the Hayashi School was a weak competitor among them. In 1789, the *bakufu*, under its chief councillor, Matsudaira Sadanobu (1758–1829), issued a proscription on heterodox ideas. But the proscription could not be imposed systematically throughout the country, and its primary purpose was really to assure that bureaucrats serving the *bakufu* were trained with a consistent set of ethical ideas.

Despite the absence of a political "orthodoxy" in the *baku-han* system, it is meaningful to speak of a set of prevailing ideas that formed an "ideology" for Tokugawa bureaucratism, whether in the *bakufu* or in each *han*.

To begin with there was an acceptance throughout the various schools of thought of the Tokugawa *baku-han* system as a historically legitimate form of government. Developed over the previous five centuries, this was a decentralized form of rule, rendered as *hōken*, the term later to be translated in the nineteenth century as "feudal," but meaning in the Tokugawa context government based on ties of interpersonal trust. It was identified explicitly with the history of preimperial China and especially the ancient Chou dynasty (ca. 1122–770 B.C.), thus giving it an added aura of legitimacy despite the obvious contrasts with China's more brilliant and symmetrical forms of *centralized* imperial rule in the later dynasties. Chinese history, it was argued by Arai Hakuseki (1657–1725), Dazai Shundai, and others, developed from decentralized to centralized imperial rule, while Japan followed a reverse process of constructing centralized government first and then decentralized forms of rule of which the Tokugawa *bakufu* marked a culmination. The point of this exercise in comparative history obviously was to emphasize Japanese history as equally legitimate to China's, thus confirming the existing system of *bakufu* government.[7]

[7] See my essay, "Political Economism in the Thought of Dazai Shundai (1680–1747)," *The Journal of Asian Studies* 31, no. 4 (August 1972): 821–39.

Of greater ideological significance, however, was the convergence of two theoretically disparate definitions of bureaucracy into an ideology supporting the *baku-han* system. Although the definitions also contained iconoclastic possibilities, their primary contribution to Tokugawa bureaucratic culture was their confirmation of the validity of loyal action within the *baku-han* system.

One of these formulations is identified with Yamazaki Ansai and his peculiar understanding and use of Neo-Confucian thought, which is generally traced to the thinker Chu Hsi (1130–1200) and which provided the basis of intellectual orthodoxy through China's later dynasties. Staunch supporters of the *bakufu* and *han* government were strongly influenced by Yamazaki, two outstanding examples being Asami Keisai (1652–1711) and Satō Naokata (1650–1719). The other conceptual position is attributable to Ogyū Sorai and more generally to a utilitarian school associated with "ancient studies" (*kogaku*) which included Yamago Sokō (1622–85) and Itō Jinsai. Students of Chinese history will readily associate the ideas of Ogyū with the tradition of legalist thought in China, although Ogyū vigorously denied this and defended himself as being true to Confucianism. Often traced to the great thinker Hsun-tzu (ca. 300–237 B.C.), and his student Han-Fei-tzu (d. 233 B.C.), the ideas of legalism were looked upon with opprobrium through much of Chinese history as being heterodox and unacceptable. Ogyū, as soon will be discussed, provided fresh and provocative expression to some of these concepts, imposing on them a powerful cogency that had far reaching significance for Japanese political history.

The two systems of thought attributed to Yamazaki and Ogyū differed greatly in their assumptions about ethical and political action, and general historical accounts in Japan and the West tend to emphasize their conflicting intellectual positions. That great and bitter debates took place between proponents of each position cannot be denied. Yet, on closer observation, elements from each were extracted and made to blend and converge into a functional "ideology" which, through much of the Tokugawa period, was used to legitimate the *baku-han* system.[8]

Yamazaki's ideas were based on two important convictions: an argument for the normative or fixed basis of political and social structures and a belief in dynamic personality.[9] The first argument, as is well known, was drawn from the logic of Neo-Confucianism, which Yamazaki shared with the Hayashi School. According to this theory, men perceive through "devoted observation" of categories of things a patterned regularity, which, through logical extension, is everywhere true. There is an "inevitable" essence or "reason" that defines things and which human "will" cannot change into something else. This argument for universal essences logically necessitates higher or more inclusive levels of universals, culminating in a universal of all universals—the great ultimate. Being constant, predictable, nonarbitrary, this universal essence is "good," transcendent of the world of evil, physical corruption, and change. Through this sequence of reasoning Yamazaki argued that the ethical nature of politics is conceivable only in the light of fixed, nonarbitrary norms outside of historical processes that make it possible for men to establish rules, rituals, and

---

[8] The term "orthodoxy" is often used to describe Tokugawa political ideology, meaning primarily Neo-Confucianism. This is misleading. The *bakufu* did not have a bureaucratic apparatus to enforce an orthodoxy and its own ideology was quite eclectic. That the conflicting views of Yamazaki Ansai and Ogyū Sorai should converge as ideology, therefore, is not as curious a point of view as students of Japanese history might think at first glance. See Bitō, *Nihon hōken shisōshi kenkyū,* pp. 17–38; Tahara, *Tokugawa shisōshi kenkyū,* pp. 7–22; Maruyama, *Nihon seiji shisōshi kenkyū* pp. 20–70; and Nagata Hiroshi, *Nihon tetsugaku shisōshi,* 2 vols. (Tokyo: Hōsei daigaku shuppankyoku, 1967), vol. 1, pp. 57–106.

[9] For Yamazaki and one of his principal disciples, Satō Naokata, see Bitō's *Nihon hōken shisōshi,* pp. 40–134, and "Hoken rinri," Iwanami kōza, *Nihon rekishi,* vol. 10, pp. 306–12. Good coverage is found in Inoue Tetsujirō, *Nihon shushigakuha no tetsukaku,* pp. 363–456. Although somewhat outdated, the following are also useful: Denki gakkai, ed., *Yamazaki Ansai to sono monryū* (Tokyo: Meiji shobō, 1943); and Kobayashi Kenzō, *Suika Shintō no kenkyū* (Tokyo: Shibundō, 1940). See also Ryusaki Tsunoda, Wm. Theodore de Bary, and Donald Keene, eds., *Sources of the Japanese Tradition* (New York: Columbia University Press, 1958), pp. 363–71.

structures. Rules and structures, in short, are visible manifestations of metaphysical norm to Yamazaki and his followers. Theirs was a canonical view of ethical and sumptuary rules that verged on religious fanaticism. Rules must be constantly reiterated, as they might be done in a religious order that demanded recitation of scripture.

There is, however, another side to Yamazaki that must be stressed. This is his view of action, or the externalization of righteousness. While fixed norms are essential for ethical politics, these norms do not determine the potential or quality of performance. Indeed, performance varies from person to person and is directly connected with his "mind," or inner mystery, his "godlike character" (*kami*), or internal power. What Yamazaki stressed, then, was not so much internal devotion to enable one to perceive ethical norms, since norms are explicit and given, but rather the indefinable potential in human personality to act out one's convictions in a public context and thereby make history approximate norms of goodness. His use of imagery is interesting too, for he sees this potential to perform as dynamic; for example, as mind transforming soil into metal, manipulating and transforming "things" in time without in any way challenging conceptually the normative foundations of all things and human structures.

Yamazaki's theory of action is intriguing from another point of view. The godlike power in men of which he speaks is clearly drawn from the indigenous Shintō tradition. Men and gods belong to undifferentiated categories; and men, as with a spirit of nature, can transform themselves into something extraordinary. The most persuasive symbol of this tradition was the Japanese emperor, man as god-king in a continuous history.

Yamazaki's legacy clearly is as ambiguous as it is complex. On one hand, the emphasis on canonical certainty of political and ethical norms provided unequivocal support of the *bakufu* despite its cumbersome structure and its sticky array of sumptuary codes and harshly punitive laws. But, on the other hand, there was also the emphasis on self-transforming activism rather than

studious devotion, in which the primary psychological identification was with the distant imperial institution, not with the immediate structure of power. The monarchy represented the purest
manifestation of metaphysical norm. For historical reasons, it
stood outside the arena of structured politics and bureaucratic
action, and symbolized, by its inactivity, the normative constant
for active self-development.

It was this view of the imperial institution as the highest historical evidence of metaphysical norm that allowed activists of
the mid-nineteenth century to view structures and existing codes
as "things," manipulable, as against norm, which is not. These
activists would remember Yamazaki not for his unequivocal confirmation of the *baku-han* system, but for his psychological identification with the monarchy as a normative symbol of loyalty.
The contradiction is evident throughout the eighteenth century
and can be detected even in Muro Kyūso (1658–1734), perhaps
the most ardent supporter of the *bakufu* on grounds of Neo-
Confucian theory of metaphysical norm. During the vendetta
incident of 1702, in which the forty-seven *rōnin* acted out of
loyalty to "lord" against *bakufu* "law," Muro was intellectually
ambivalent in his dual commitment to existing structures as fixed
entities and to the principle of loyalty as a timeless norm.[10]

It would seem that Neo-Confucian theory by itself could not
have provided a stable "ideology" for the *bakufu*. Although the
term "Neo-Confucian" is often used to describe that ideology,
there was also strong reinforcement from a separate, theoretical

---

[10] Muro Kyūso compiled a record in 1730 of the forty-seven-*rōnin* incident (*Akō gijin roku*, 2 vols.). Although a loyal defender of the *baku-han*
system and all of its rules and laws, Muro expressed deep admiration for the
rōnin because of their commitment to the principle of loyalty, even though
they had clearly violated *bakufu* law in carrying out the vendetta. It is also
interesting to note that while Muro is often cited as the most "orthodox" of
the Neo-Confucian ideologues for the *bakufu*, he turned to Neo-Confucianism
quite late in life and is said to have had leanings toward an idealism traceable
to the Ōyōmei or Wang Yang-ming tradition. Some of Muro's writings are
reprinted in Araki Kengo and Inoue Tadashi, eds., *Nihon shisō taikei*, vol. 34,
Kaibara Ekken, Muro Kyūso (Tokyo: Iwanami shoten, 1970): see especially
Araki's essay on Muro's thought, pp. 505–30.

orientation. This reinforcement came from the school of "ancient studies," which included a number of outstanding thinkers such as Yamaga Sokō, Itō Jinsai, Ogyū Sorai, and Dazai Shundai.[11] All of them shared certain common assumptions. They all rejected a priori norms as theoretical premises upon which to structure ethics and politics. They also rejected Neo-Confucian dualism, the explanation of the natural and social order as a balance between mind and matter, essence and shape. They all started from a materialistic monism, viewing existence and the universe in terms of a single life principle and then proceeded from that monism to explain ethical and social structures as extensions of concrete human need. In the critique of Yamaga Sokō, the underlying fallacy of Neo-Confucianism is its failure to distinguish between "thing" (*mono*) and "fact" (*koto*): "Thing" always precedes "fact," the former is physical reality, the latter is experienced activity. In short "fact" is not of the order of "things" and belongs to the human realm of idea and action. These activities take place within structures of power, and their repetition over time is called "custom" and "history." [12]

It was Ogyū Sorai, however, who was by far the outstanding political thinker and who provided the most thoroughgoing theory of bureaucracy based on social utility.[13] Reminiscent of legal-

---

[11] Tahara, *Tokugawa shisōshi kenkyū*, deals with Yamaga Sokō, Ogyū Sorai, and Itō Jinsai in considerable depth, while Imanaka Kanji, *Soraigaku no kisoteki kenkyū* (Tokyo: Yoshikawa kōbunkan, 1966), goes into a wide variety of Ogyū's writings. See also Bitō Masahide, "Itō Jinsai ni okeru gakumon to jissen," *Shisō* 2, no. 524 (1968): 66–79; and Maeda Ichirō, "Keiken kagaku no tanjō," *Iwanami kōza, Nihon rekishi*, vol. 11, *Kinsei, 3* (Tokyo: Iwanami shoten, 1963), pp. 171–214, esp. pp. 173–84.

[12] Bitō, "Hōken rinri," Iwanami kōza, *Nihon rekishi*, vol. 10, pp. 300–306 and also his essay on Japanese Confucianism, "Jukyo," in Bitō, ed., *Nihon bunka to Chūgoku*, pp. 172–87, esp. pp. 180–83.

[13] Translations in English of some of Ogyū's writings are J. R. McEwan, *The Political Writings of Ogyū Sorai* (London: Cambridge University Press, 1962); and Olof G. Lidin, *Ogyū Sorai's Distinguishing the Way* (Tokyo: Sophia University Press, 1970). The basic writings of Ogyū, *Bendō, Bemmei*, and *Tōmonsho* can be found in a number of different collections of Tokugawa thought as in *Nihon rinri ihen*, 10 vols. (Tokyo: Ikuseikai, 1901), esp. vol. 6. In recent years they have begun to appear in collected works of Ogyū: Maru-

ist thought in Chinese history, Ogyū stressed the importance of bureaucratic codes, or "law," in human society, over abstract ethical concepts. Ogyū proceeded with a criticism of Itō Jinsai, who had wavered between a materialistic principle of "life," or the constant activity of things, as the only reality with which to build ethics, and a concept of human "goodness," which Itō documented with the ideas of Mencius. For Itō, however, this "goodness" was not innate or methaphysical but an ethical possibility toward which men might aspire. Ogyū found Itō's theory faulty because it did not make explicit the relationship between ethics, or the concept of goodness, and political hierarchy. Fundamental to all historical processes, Ogyū argued with much bombast, is that "power" precedes "ethics." It is concrete bureaucratic "constructs" that are creative extensions of men, not abstract "ethics," as Itō tended to argue. Political hierarchies are fabrications based on human and social need; ethics are merely bureaucratic rules and regulations, what the ancients called "ritual," that give structures coherence and regularity in the exercise of power.

Ogyū's argument was provocative. Political institutions were not "fixed" according to timeless metaphysical norm, as Yamazaki Ansai and others believed, they were "made." Ethics were not abstract universals, nor was the emperor a manifestation of the principle of loyalty. Ethics were rational because they were used with political intent. In the broadest sense, this intent meant providing peace and economic well-being for society (*ammin*).

The truth about the rationality of ethics and politics, Ogyū reasoned, could be understood through the study of history. Indeed, history was the highest form of knowledge men could attain —*gakumon wa rekishi ni kiwamari sōrō*—because it explained the basis of social existence. History showed that the ancient kings and sages of China created political society, built hierarchies and

---

yama Masao, Yoshikawa Kojirō, Nishida Taichirō and Tsuji Tatsuya, eds., *Nihon shisō taikei*, vol. 36, *Ogyū Sorai* (Tokyo: Iwanami shoten, 1973); and Imanaka Kanji and Naramoto Tatsuya, eds., *Ogyū Sorai zenshū*, 8 vols., (Tokyo: Kawade shobō, 1973–   ). The most provocative work on Ogyū Sorai is still Maruyama's *Nihon seiji shisōshi kenkyū*.

regulated them with "rituals," all to mediate relations *between* men and not to discover the ultimates of metaphysical principles. With their creation of institutional and social norms, the "way of men" and the "way of nature," social and natural "things," were irrevocably split. Ethics were not of nature but of the social order. The principles governing the natural order could not be totally understood; those which govern society could be studied, documented, applied.

The implications of Ogyū's political theory were clear. The existing *baku-han* system of bureaucracy was legitimate. Ethics within the system might be thought of as a complex of punitive, regulative, and sumptuary codes designed to provide order and well-being. It had been created by great men, Ieyasu and his advisers, to solve concrete social problems, notably the need for peace. Loyalty within the present context was not to "principle" but to "law." Yet, like any other set of historical constructions, the *baku-han* system was not metaphysically sacrosanct, and therefore its longevity was dependent on its capacity to respond continuously to changing historical needs. Confirmation of structure was not to be achieved through recitation of canonical scripture, but in careful and systematic study of the relation between politics and history and in making prescriptions as to how the political system should respond. In short, having provided a theory of history and social ethics to confirm the existing *baku-han* system, Ogyū injected a principle of "utility" that was logical to his conceptual framework and that placed the burden of continuing legitimation on the performance of the system itself.

This principle of utility was given new significance by Dazai Shundai, an outstanding follower of Ogyū.[14] Political systems, Dazai reasoned, must respond to the environment and to social passion. The latter in particular was especially difficult to assess because passion, while inevitable to all men, expressed itself according to economic groups. Thus, one might speak of the "passion of merchants" in contrast to the "passion of *samurai* and

[14] Najita, "Political Economism in the Thought of Dazai," pp. 830–35.

peasants." Each of these social categories rested on different principles of accruing wealth. Viewing his own political and economic universe, Dazai concluded that the *baku-han* system must incorporate into its process of governance the principle of exchange or trade upon which the merchants relied. To assure strength and survival, each *han* ought to involve itself in vigorous multiregional trade and systematically accumulate wealth without regard to conventional ethical proscriptions.

Although working within Ogyū's theoretical framework, Dazai went beyond the agrarianism to which Ogyū was committed. The only "absolute" in history for Dazai was the principle that political constructs must respond effectively to social needs. Social and political continuity depended on this responsive capacity. His optimism about the *baku-han* system faltered on occasion. Still, he, too, wrote to justify the existence of that system and to prescribe action that would assure its survival.

In viewing Yamazaki Ansai on the one hand and Ogyū Sorai (and Dazai) on the other, certain contrasts are plainly evident. In Yamazaki, heavy emphasis is placed on the interior capacity of men to act relative to norms and structures that are fixed in accordance with metaphysical theory. There is constancy in history that makes social existence predictable and ethical. The dynamic factor, however, is the individual and his capacity to act, transform things, display his righteousness in a social and bureaucratic context. It is a system of thought that confirms the *samurai* ethic of devoted service and provides it with bureaucratic and metaphysical certainty.

Ogyū and Dazai stand in contrast to Yamazaki. Both men deemphasize the interior capacity of men, bureaucrats and otherwise, to generate goodness from within vis à vis fixed ethical norms. They deny metaphysical constancy in history and in institutions. "Truths" documented in the classics are merely "language," not evidence of an unchanging goodness. Above all, the key variable is not the individual but political constructs: What is decisive is not the *geist* in human personality, but fabricated political norms embedded in objective structures to regulate relations between men. The loyal servitor, therefore, is not one who seeks goodness or spiritual power in the self, but the one who seeks to make structures responsive to changing social needs. Ogyū's "hero" is of a different sort from Yamazaki's. In ordinary times, he formulates rational prescriptions for the existing system to solve specific social problems; in extraordinary times, he theoretically creates systems *de novo* (as Ieyasu did with the *baku-han* system). Throughout, however, Ogyū maintains the view that bureaucracy is essential to social existence.

The theoretical differences between the two modes of bureaucratic thought, then, are profound. Yet, despite these differences, they also converge and reinforce each other as an ideology. Both are normative systems of thought. For Yamazaki, ultimate norm is outside of history, although, as mentioned earlier, the imperial institution is looked upon as the original point at which metaphysical norm becomes a historical constant. For Ogyū, norm is in history and not in the emperor as an abstract principle. The "monarch" is merely the terminal point of secular hierarchy; it symbolizes the truth that all hierarchies of power must have an end. There is, however, a normative principle in history that does not change, and which therefore is a functional absolute: Regardless of time, place, and circumstance, bureaucratic structures are necessary for social existence, for the realization of such practical ends as domestic peace, orderly economic life, and, later, national autonomy. Ethics and all known concepts of "goodness" rest on this pragmatic principle underlying bureaucratic constructs. This principle is identical with the pragmatic *intent* behind the formation of social rituals by the ancient kings when they first created society; and it will live on as an absolute in history.

However disparate in theory, both Yamazaki and Ogyū's premises pointed to a conception of political structures as "absolute." Both premises confirmed the existing system and, in this sense, legitimated the feudal order. In short, whether argued from metaphysical premises or historical and functional ones, the Tokugawa *baku-han* system could be explained and accepted as a framework for ethical and practical action. Neither system of thought allowed leeway for piecemeal tampering with parts of the structure. Norms and structures must be "absolute," both positions held, because the alternative was arbitrary reliance on physical power, which constrained effective action. Ideology, therefore, must be "consistent" (more so than being "true") so that structures might perform in predictable ways. This view of structural absolutism resulted in a theoretical eclecticism (*setchū-gaku*) in which Ogyū Sorai's ideas about the pragmatic character of secular social organization were used to incorporate, on functional grounds, the metaphysical and psychological ethics of Yamazaki Ansai's Neo-Confucianism. The efforts of *bakufu* leaders such as the chief councillor Matsudaira Sadanobu to establish an "orthodox" ideology were pinned to this eclectic tendency.[15] Matsudaira, who drew heavily from the intellectual tradition of Yamazaki for his specific ethical views, defended the use of that tradition as an "orthodoxy" as against "heterodoxy" (as defined in the proscription on heterodoxy of 1790) with the pragmatic argument that the *bakufu* as a bureaucratic system needed a functional ideological absolute. He derived this functional theory about political ethics from Ogyū.

The intellectual concern with the problem of structural absolutism continued into the nineteenth century, and it took an ironic twist, especially with the impingement of Western power in the 1850s. The existing bureaucratic order, it was argued, was not sufficiently "absolute." It was held together with the threat of physical force and not by "fixed norms" (*teihō*), thus making the system arbitrary and oppressive to men with good intentions to act effectively.

This criticism that the *bakufu* was not responsive to norm

15 The school of eclectics is discussed in Inukasa Yasuki, "Setchūgakuha no seiji oyobi gakumon shisō," *Nihonshi kenkyū* 40, no. 2 (1959): 29–39, and 41, no. 3 (1959): 28–49. The same author has also written "Setchūgakuha to kyōgaku tōsei," *Iwanami kōza, Nihon rekishi*, vol. 12, *kinsei, 4* (Tokyo: Iwanami shoten, 1963), pp. 199–232. Maruyama discusses the relationship between Ogyū's thought and *bakufu* ideology in *Nihon seiji shisōshi*, pp. 145–47 and 283–85.

also developed out of the mixture of Yamazaki and Ogyū. With slight reworking, both systems of thought could be applied to the evaluation of existing structures in light of what they ought more properly to be. Ideology, in short, could be reshaped into criticism of existing politics and its immediate history.

This iconoclastic mixture is readily evident in the thought of Yamagata Daini (1725–67), the critic of the *bakufu* executed for his outspoken views.[16] Drawing on Ogyū, Yamagata stripped the *bakufu* of the pretension of timeless certitude. He retained, however, Ogyū's insistence on the need for explicit norms on utilitarian grounds. Bureaucratic structures, Yamagata speculated, were fabricated extensions of human need, and the *bakufu* ought to be assessed and held accountable in the light of empirical social needs. Yamagata pointed especially to the obvious contradiction between unremitting poverty in the countryside and the arbitrary use of power to maintain the pomp and luxury of the upper *samurai* elite. While pursuing this line of argument, however, Yamagata also retained Yamazaki Ansai's notion of "imperial justice" as a metaphysically fixed norm symbolized by the emperor. This focus on the imperial institution as the point at which metaphysical norm becomes immanent, allowed Yamagata to separate objective structures from "norm" and to urge "rectification" of the present, using "imperial justice" as a metaphysical constant. In short, structures could be unmade and remade, as Ogyū taught, but the monarchy was not an extension of political reality. It was a referent point of a metaphysical "value" outside of the structured confines of "action."

In Yamagata, two sets of normative concepts, metaphysical and historical, converge on the imperial institution. Timeless norm and the ultimate political sanction of hierarchy combine in ambiguous fashion to define the character of the Japanese emperor. It is in this convergence that the political "rediscovery" of the emperor in middle and late Tokugawa Japan takes on his-

[16] See my essay, "Restorationism in the Political Thought of Yamagata Daini (1725–67)," *The Journal of Asian Studies* 31, no. 1 (November 1971): 17–29.

torical significance. Yet perhaps what needs to be emphasized is not the political iconoclasm for which this imperial ideology, without much difficulty, could be reassembled and used. Of greater ideological importance is that as the monarchical symbol steadily gained stature as a normative entity in the ethical sense, a counter tendency developed to define existing bureaucratic structures as functional absolutes and, in this sense, "relative"; to perceive them as a pragmatic framework for action and as a hierarchy of power and less as structured embodiments of timeless and inevitable truths. This tendency is not iconoclastic as in Yamagata Daini's sweeping denial of the political present. It is supportive of bureaucratic "action" within functional constructs. It emphasizes the pragmatic content and the calculated impact of bureaucratic action as taking precedence over an identification with normative essence: *na yori mo jitsu,* or "pragmatic content over form," a dictum regularly repeated in both late Tokugawa and modern Japan.

The ideological justification of bureaucratic action repeated competently and with dedication over time is without question a central political legacy of Tokugawa feudalism. It is a legacy that combines structured activity by a bureaucratic aristocracy with articulate thinking about the validity and limits of bureaucratic and ethical action. As indicated in this chapter, there is clear evidence of the conscious employment of metaphysical and historical ideas to sanction loyal bureaucratic action, to make the *baku-han* system, once established and fixed into place, work effectively and with purpose. There is also a conviction of the human capacity for rational and disciplined perception (*kei*). Ethical political action, therefore, must be linked to the human potential for rational bureaucratic perception, the capacity to see relationships between self and structures and structures and time, and to prescribe action accordingly. There is here an awareness of tactic, timing, and of necessary limitations imposed by normative structures.

Yet what gives added complexity to the Tokugawa political legacy is a concurrent theme of idealistic skepticism regarding the claims of objectivity and rationality in bureaucratic ideology. In this idealistic tradition, devoted cultivation of rational perception is criticized as leading to self-understanding only in terms of what exists externally in structures of power and knowledge. Action may confirm what exists, but what exists need not be ethical or just. Together with bureaucratic ideology, this idealistic tradition constitutes a crucial dimension in the ethics of action (*kōdō* and *jissen rinri*) in Tokugawa Japan. Both these themes are woven into a mode of thought and action called "restorationism," which is the subject of our next chapter. It was within this conceptual framework of "restorationism" that the Tokugawa order would be destroyed, and through which, paradoxically, Tokugawa theories of action would outlive the feudal structures within which they had been formulated and continue as important forces into the modern era.

3

Restorationism in Late Tokugawa

The Meiji Restoration of 1868 completely dismantled the Tokugawa political order and replaced it with a centralized system of government under the emperor. An iconoclastic event, the Meiji Restoration is decisive in the emergence of Japan as a modern nation. It marks the culmination of the rise of strident criticism and protest voiced in the language of "restorationism" that began in the late Tokugawa period.

Although "restorationism" did not express itself in a nationally organized movement, it steadily gained intelligibility in the early nineteenth century as a pragmatic and moral critique against the *bakufu*. It challenged the *bakufu*'s "homeostatic" inflexibility in the light of disturbances within the country and from abroad, and provided the conceptual framework that allowed Japan to develop in a totally new direction.

For the historian, then, "restorationism" provides a focus for widely disparate events spanning some fifty years between 1840 and 1890, with the Meiji Restoration as the high point. In these years, a particular flow of history was irreversibly altered and channeled into a generically new course of development. Agrarian,

43

semicentralized, aristocratic, and seclusionist in 1800, Japan in 1900 was unmistakenly industrial, centralized, egalitarian, constitutional, and expansionist. As with Peter Laslett's perception of England during the industrial transformation,[1] a world was lost in those one hundred years in Japan. The key political perspective, without question, is "restorationism."

Restorationism was grounded in Tokugawa political thought. As was observed in the previous chapter, institutional utility was a key principle in Tokugawa thought. Political constructs, in this view, must be tested according to historical need, metaphysical ethic, or a flexible combination of both. If bureaucratic instruments were demonstrably unworkable, loyal men ought to respond to the problem. Through the eighteenth century, this response came in the form of more effective prescriptions for bureaucratic performance. Planted in this discourse, however, was the conceptualization (traceable to Ogyū Sorai and his school) that political systems were not sacrosanct and that "sages" could "restore" and potentially "create" *de novo* alternative structures, the alternative most often referred to being "centralized government," or *gun-ken seido.*

To this utilitarian view was added a crucial theory of political action that viewed bureaucratic reason and existing ideology with deep philosophical skepticism. It sought a basis for true and loyal commitment (*chū*) without the constraining influences of hierarchy. The medieval value of true loyalty remained important to the Tokugawa *samurai,* and it grew in intellectual and political importance in the latter half of the Tokugawa period, especially as bureaucratic structure and ideology gained the appearance of being unassailably entrenched. This value of true loyalty was often expressed in the language of philosophical idealism or of national historicism.

What the Meiji Restoration of 1868 added as the pivotal event in the development of "restorationism" was a compelling

---

[1] Peter Laslett, *The World We Have Lost* (New York: Charles Scribner's Sons, 1965).

reorientation toward the problems of institutional utility and of designing structured efficiency based on new "constants." The prior intervening impacts of idealistic action, however, were crucial. Throughout the years leading to the Meiji Restoration, there was a powerful undercurrent of iconoclasm, of a readiness to identify with the "divine" over existing "virtue," which, in retrospect, gave new historical outlet to the principle of utility and bureaucratic rationality beyond the confining framework of feudal constructs.

The precise manner in which these two modes of thought and action combined into criticism is extremely difficult to trace. They were not neatly documented in a manifesto or a formal treatise on political revolt. The language was not specialized, as critical political language tends to be in the modern era, but intelligible in a diffuse manner throughout Tokugawa political culture. No single group of persons had a monopoly on these ideas. Indeed, all the principal actors of this history, whether within the *bakufu* or outside and opposed to it, were familiar with these two critical positions of idealistic action and institutional utility and were influenced by both of them in varying degrees. Often cited for its influence is the synthetic thought of late Mito studies. Although eclectic in content, it initiated openly from "within" the Tokugawa political and ideological order a pragmatic criticism against the *bakufu*, legitimating itself ultimately on loyalty to the imperial institution. The idealistic critique is best seen in the intellectual tradition of Ōyōmei (the Japanese reading of Wang Yang-ming, 1472–1529) and in the development of national studies (*kokugaku*).

THE MITO CRITIQUE

Mito was a collateral *han* of the ruling Tokugawa house. Assigned the task by the *bakufu* of compiling a comprehensive history of Japan, Mito developed in the latter half of the Tokugawa period into an impressive academic fief, attracting leading scholars of the day. Going well beyond the compilation of history,

Mito developed an eclectic framework within which to discuss political ideology and power relations. Its principal writers in the early nineteenth century were Aizawa Seishisai (1782–1863) and Fujita Tōko (1806–55). Their ideas, first applied to politics by the young *daimyō* of Mito, Tokugawa Nariaki (1800–1860), to gain an advantage in *bakufu* politics, later became important conceptual weapons for critics of the *bakufu*. Aizawa was especially well known, and loyal activists from throughout the country (such as Yoshida Shōin [1830–59] from distant Chōshū) made a special point of calling on him at a strategic point in their careers.

Mito thought developed within the legitimate confines of Tokugawa bureaucratic ideology.[2] At its core was a dualism reminiscent of Yamazaki Ansai's ideas. There was a strong identification with the imperial institution as a pure cultural ideal. There was also a general theoretical framework that was normative in the Neo-Confucian sense of "names" having a metaphysical reality that explain and legitimate things. Thus, the monarchical symbol was made to coincide simultaneously with history and with metaphysical norm, placing the monarchy outside the realm of actual politics and administration. Below the monarchy was the all-encompassing realm of practical management and action.

In this dualism there was initially a perception of the monarchy as a total normative ideal, pure and hence inactive, an object of faith to which ultimate loyalty is extended. Facing it was the realm of dynamic action, flexible maneuver, and practical achievement, in which, by implication, there should be greater

2 Documents of the Mito school have been compiled in massive tomes (as in Takasu Yasujirō, ed., *Mitogaku taikei*, 8 vols. (Tokyo: Mitogaku taikei kankōkai, 1940–42), and a great deal has been written about it in Japanese, especially in the prewar period. An introductory essay is Tōyama Shigeki, "Mitogaku no seikaku," in Nakamura Kōya, ed., *Seikatsu to shisō* (Tokyo: Shōgakukan, 1944), in which Tōyama places Mito thought within the established order, denying it revolutionary significance, a theme he developed further in his well-known work, *Meiji Ishin* (Tokyo: Iwanami shoten, 1951). I have stressed the view that political uncertainty within the established order developed from challenges formulated within the framework of "ideology" itself. See also Matsumoto Sannosuke, *Tennōseikokka to seijishisō* (Tokyo: Miraisha, 1969), pp. 62–72.

allowance for loyal men from Mito to make their contribution. In this realm of performance it was the utilitarian assumptions identified with the school of Ogyū Sorai that were clearly operative.

The pragmatic theme is readily apparent in Aizawa's influential work of 1825, *Shinron*, or *A New Thesis*.[3] Discussing what he believed to be the proper "techniques" of present rule, Aizawa questioned the defensive capacity of the *bakufu* as a political and social system. The encroachment of Western power throughout the Far East, he observed, was inevitable. As a matter of practical strategy, Japan must break out of its present seclusion to confront that threat. Such a strategy, however, required the mobilization of the total energy of society without regard to previous class structure. A multiclass army and navy must be formed, and modern firearms must be forged at once. Moreover, to enhance support from society, maximum use must be made of ethical and religious ideas, symbols, images, rituals, and shrines. These should all be identified with the monarchical symbol and the ideal of a continuous national historical essence (*kokutai*). The common people, in short, should not be feared, nor should they merely be controlled through punitive devices, but viewed as a source of social energy and, through the cultivation of "loyalty to the emperor" (*sonnō*), incorporated into the formation of a strong country. Here, as with the tradition of Ogyū Sorai, "loyalism" was a technique for effective rule. Its theoretical legitimation was historical need, not metaphysical essence.

Just how clearly Aizawa perceived the threat of Western power is not certain. In 1825, his perception of that threat was probably vague and inexact, a hypothetical example of the worst that might happen to threaten national survival. More than a

---

[3] See the stimulating work of my colleague, Harry D. Harootunian, *Toward Restoration* (Berkeley: University of California Press, 1970). See also Richard T. Chang, *From Prejudice to Tolerance* (Tokyo: Sophia University Press, 1970). Aizawa's *Shinron* is in paperback, *Shinron, Yūihen* (Tokyo: Iwanami shoten, 1969; first published 1931). An insightful analysis by Bitō Masahide is appended on pp. 293–312.

recognition of the imminence of Western bombardment, his ideas were a statement of the structural inflexibility of the *bakufu* regardless of the source of physical disturbance. Although not intended as a revolutionary manifesto, there was in Aizawa's *Shinron* an iconoclasm that challenged the integrity of the *bakufu*. In the event of severe crises, the argument ran, the *bakufu* would prove to be inflexible and ineffectual. Seclusionism was not a practical strategy against the West. The class structure was anachronistic, not because the *samurai* were unnecessary but because the *samurai* were not allowed to act constructively. Everyone must be made to contribute his loyal services. And the *bakufu* must link its actions more closely with the legitimating monarchical symbol. Throughout this sequence of thinking, Aizawa's intent was not to reject existing structures, but to make them perform more effectively. Yet, despite these obvious requirements, the *bakufu* did not readjust its strategies because it wished to protect its narrow basis of power; and Aizawa was compelled to touch on the question of how that power is divided—a question which carried far-reaching political implications.

Aizawa's ideas became part of the political process through the maneuvers and intrigues in Edo in the 1830s of the young *daimyō* Mito Nariaki.[4] Through Nariaki's efforts, Mito thought became widely publicized as a critique on the *bakufu*. The *daimyō* of one of the most prestigious fiefs in the country and a blood-related house of the shogun, he had indicated rather openly and brashly his displeasure with *bakufu* decision-making. The crack, however thin, proved to be irreparable. Loyal regional leaders such as himself, Nariaki argued, should be allowed greater voice in deciding national policy. He reiterated his commitment to retain the structures as they stood. The *bakufu* should remain as

---

[4] See John W. Hall and Yoshio Sakata, "The Motivation of Political Leadership in the Meiji Restoration," *The Journal of Asian Studies* 16, no. 1 (November 1956): 31–50. A discussion of this general period is found in Okamoto Ryōichi's "Tempō kaikaku," *Iwanami kōza, Nihon rekishi,* vol. 13, *Kinsei,* 5 (Tokyo: Iwanami shoten, 1964), pp. 209–50. Also useful is Rekishigaku kenkyūkai, ed., *Meiji Ishin shi kenkyū kōza,* 6 vols. (Tokyo: Heibonsha, 1958), especially vol. 2, pp. 3–31 and 117–267.

it was, which is to also say that Mito should continue as a semi-autonomous regional bastion related by blood to the Tokugawa house. But "men of talent" from Mito (and by implication elsewhere, although this point was left vague) should directly participate in decisions affecting the entire country.

Agrarian uprising, fiscal chaos, uncontrolled commercialism, the impending crisis in seclusionism, all were nationwide problems that the *bakufu* was not equipped, structurally, to solve by itself. Since the *bakufu* was committed ideologically to the existing institutional arrangement, the incorporation of regional leadership was a logical prescription. And it was legitimate because all administrative units below the imperial or "metaphysical" level of politics belonged to a common political sphere, held together by an ultimate identification of loyalty to the monarchy. Expanded flexibility in administrative strategy, therefore, might be preceded by a harmonious and virtuous coalescence of the ideal and the pragmatic, or the court and *bakufu* (*kōbugattai*), which meant, as a practical matter, the expanded reliance on impeccably "loyal" regional *daimyō* such as Mito Nariaki. Without conceding the semiautonomous status of Mito, the *daimyō* Nariaki, armed with ideas of Aizawa and others, had punctured the *bakufu's* metaphysical claims to power and reduced it in stature to an efficient administration in which Nariaki might participate.

The *bakufu* reacted quickly to Mito Nariaki. Under its chief councillor, Mizuno Tadakuni (1794–1851), the *bakufu* reaffirmed its essential features. In what is known as the Tempō Reforms (named after the Tempō period, 1830–43), self-sufficient agrarianism and seclusionism were reconfirmed. After a decree terminating commercial monopolies and allowing the free movement of goods, the *bakufu*, realizing its inability to enforce this decree, scrupulously retreated and avoided the entire question of establishing a national fiscal and currency structure. Rather than expand its bureaucratic authority and potentially intervene in the regional affairs of the *han*, or, as Mito Nariaki urged, incorporate men like himself into the *bakufu* government, the *bakufu* reaffirmed the principle of baronial autonomy as a cardinal feature of the system. This meant a clear rejection of baronial participation in the political and administrative affairs of the *bakufu*. In plain and abrupt language, Mito Nariaki was ordered to leave Edo and remain in house exile until advised otherwise; Aizawa was similarly sentenced to house exile and Fujita Tōko was imprisoned in Edo. And against the pragmatic ideas advanced by Mito scholarship, the *bakufu* restated its conviction about the timelessness of historical reason, virtue, and frugality, and of loyal service within existing structural certainties.

The insistence on the fixed character of "virtue," and hence of "power," as against "utility," came precisely at a time when such a position was being rendered untenable by events in history outside of Japan. In 1844, Mito Nariaki could be sent into house exile and even be physically coerced if he chose to resist. The same could not be done to Perry in 1853. The critique of Mito thought, therefore, continued to grow in importance regarding the demonstrable ineffectiveness of the *bakufu*, providing pragmatic and utilitarian arguments as well as emotional ones emphasizing loyal commitment to the emperor.

Yet, the *bakufu* itself was not unaware of its ineffectualness and saw a need to adapt, a point historians have often failed to discuss. It was aware of the grave economic crisis in the country, and it had more than just a sense of what kinds of action would be required to correct it. And it was the *bakufu*, after all, that discarded the seclusionist policy in the 1850s on pragmatic grounds. Its affirmations of its own organization and of existing "virtue" were neither mechanical acts nor blind belief in metaphysical truths, as historians sometimes imply, but rationally calculated decisions to preserve a political system. In restrospect, the *bakufu*'s failure to adapt to the threat from abroad resulted less from a lack of internal intelligence, which it certainly had, than from forces within the country which would not allow it to adapt in terms of its own political needs and self-conception.

In short, the *bakufu* was attacked from within. Observable through the 1840s and steadily mounting in the 1850s was a provocative willingness by critics of the *bakufu* to break with previous ties and commitments and to resist the decisions being made by the *bakufu*. This idealistic activism, added to the utilitarian perception, gave rise to acts of extreme iconoclasm against the *bakufu* and shook its sense of political self-confidence. Central to the intellectual makeup of this iconoclasm was a mixture of philosophical and nationalistic idealism. Together, they made up an important tradition of viewing political activism as being in theoretical contrast to bureaucratic and utilitarian ideology and deserve special attention as a vital part of the radical content of "restorationism" in the late Tokugawa period.

IDEALISM AS ETHIC OF ACTION: ŌYŌMEI AND NATIONAL STUDIES

A number of distinct yet overlapping intellectual tendencies are discernible in late Tokugawa idealism. Rejected is the view that the devoted observation of things can tell what personal commitment ought to be: Observation, whether with metaphysical or historical perspective, can explain what structures are, but not what is true; it can confirm historical knowledge, but not clarify institutional failings; it tells why men conform to bureaucratic norms, but not why men ought to act ethically. A romantic view of human personality is plainly evident: Spiritual ideal is emphasized over structure, status, scholarship, self-interest; faith supersedes reason as does loyal action over meditation. History, moreover, is not seen as rationally patterned, as being predictable according to a cosmic ethical scheme. History is either the unfolding of moral spirit that trenscends conventional reason, or it is divine, a creation of "gods" and hence beyond mechanical, bureaucratic control. There is here a belief in possibility of the miraculous happening in history, of social imperfections and misery being totally corrected and rectified. Above all, it is a tradition that demands action based on faith in what one believes to be true irrespective of objective barriers.

This perspective is vital to the understanding of the psychology of political anger, defiance, and rebellious activism that is woven into the eclectic intellectual structure of Japanese political history. The two modes of thought and action that stand out in this intellectual tradition are theoretically disparate: Ōyōmei idealism is a philosophy about the ultimate essence of the cosmos; national studies, or *kokugaku*, is a historical concept of the distinctiveness of Japanese culture. Yet they reinforce each other, in late Tokugawa history, with their common emphasis on the ultimately intuitional nature of political action. In this regard, they stand in contrast to the bureaucratic ideas advanced by Yamazaki Ansai and Ogyū Sorai.

Ōyōmei studies developed outside the discourse on the theoretical underpinning of the *baku-han* system. It focused itself on the intellectual point at which structured knowledge and bureaucratic reason end. For Nakae Tōju (1608–48),[5] the first thinker to concentrate on this problem of action, the philological documentation of history and the encyclopedic collection of plants and grasses, as practiced by Kaibara Ekken (1630–1714) and others, were limited by a reliance on "rational" perception. In fact, what is true cannot be "structured," documented into "codes," or "fixed" in conventional ways. This view was logical. If principle is absolute, timeless, and pervades the universe, as Nakae reasoned, then it cannot be conditioned by historical perceptions and structures. It is intelligible according to one's inner intuitive power. Men have at their immediate disposal only the wisdom of received knowledge, custom, and social institutions. But this accumulation of historical knowledge should not be confused with what is ethically true and what are proper actions.

Nakae, in his quest for spiritual autonomy, departed from status and bureaucratic service. Although not a "revolutionary," he no longer accepted the political definition of "virtue" and looked for true commitment outside the framework of competi-

---

[5] Bitō, *Nihon hōken shisōshi*, pp. 136–216, and "Hōken rinri," pp. 294–300. A general coverage is in Inoue, *Yōmeigakuha*, pp. 1–187. The most detailed work on Nakae is Gotō Saburō, *Nakae Tōju kenkyū*, 3 vols. (Tokyo: Risōsha, 1969–70).

tive bureaucratic performance. Severing ties with officialdom and scholarly academics, Nakae sought to rediscover a sense of personal ideal and potential by turning to a simpler and more humane existence, totally dedicating himself to helping the plight of lowly farmers.

Nakae (and his disciple Kumazawa Banzan, 1619–91),[6] became cultural heroes in the Tokugawa period. They retained the profound respect of scholars who believed in the necessity of hierarchy and in the importance of historical scholarship and were revered by commoners for their humane concern for the poor. They came to be idealized for their refusal to retire into a sanctuary to write poetic laments about the world of decline and decadence. They were true heroes of the Tokugawa period (in contrast to Ogyū Sorai for example who was not), and were remembered well into the modern period for their conscious rejection of bureaucratic politics.

Perhaps of greater significance, they were important in the education of the *samurai*. Although trained to become bureaucrats, all *samurai* were instructed in the Ōyōmei principle of action. This principle held that at critical points in one's life (and by extension, of society's as well) conventional reason and perceptions may not be helpful guidelines to action and that in these moments, one must reach deeply into his spiritual self and commit himself decisively to a course of action because he believes that course to be right, not because it might be advantageous. Nakae and Kumazawa were frequently used examples to reinforce this intuitional theory of action. Virtually every *samurai*, regardless of ultimate intellectual identification, be it with Neo-Confucianism, ancient studies, the school of eclecticism, or national studies, went through an "Ōyōmei phase" and incorporated its message, especially as embodied in Nakae and Kumazawa, to prepare himself for the possibility of unexpected contingency.

[6] Bitō, *Nihon hōken shisōshi,* pp. 217–76. There is also Gotō Yōichi and Tomoeda Ryūtarō, eds., *Nihon shisōshi taikei,* vol. 30, *Kumazawa Banzan* (Tokyo: Iwanami shoten, 1971).

What was taught to every *samurai* to reconfirm the ethic of selfless loyalty potentially could be turned into a denunciation of existing politics. The possibility was implicit in Nakae and in Satō Issai (1772–1859), who ostensibly trained bureaucrats in Neo-Confucian ideology as head of the *bakufu* college, but who gained nationwide fame for his private lectures on Ōyōmei idealism. It was with Ōshio Heihachirō (1793–1837), however, that the iconoclasm in Ōyōmei thought was turned into a strident rejection of the present. The quiet cultivation of inner strength for possible contingency was deemphasized. In the light of pervasive misery, contingency was in the present. In Ōshio, quietism was transformed into active revolt on behalf of the downtrodden.[7]

As with Nakae, Ōshio proceeded from an idealistic monism. It was defined as an a priori principle transcendent of time, historical reason, and scholarship. Being intelligible through intuition alone, the absolute redefined the true self as essentially "selfless," capable of total objectivity in ethical action. Ogyū Sorai and Dazai Shundai, it will be recalled, denied this argument of human personality, arguing that passion was inevitable to the self, a fact that necessitated hierarchy and bureaucratic norms. For Ōshio, such an argument concealed the great gap that existed between one's ethical potential and the structured exercise of power. All historical structures must be seen as relative to moral principle, not as generic extensions of it, as taught by Neo-Confucian scholars. The perception of this truth required separation of the self from structures and an identification with, or return to, the absolute universal ideal (*kitaikyō*).

In Ōshio, the principle of personal autonomy was redefined to mean social action. The quest for true self was in rendering public every act of self-clarification. Objective events and subjective activities were coincidental: the rectification of evil in the self *ipso facto* meant action against injustice in society. In short, Nakae's departure from structures to return to the soil became Ōshio's action against those structures that perpetuate injustice and social misery.

For Ōshio, a low-ranking official for the *bakufu* in the city of Osaka, this defiance expressed itself besides the impetuous manners for which he was well known) in the surreptitious collection and forging of guns. In 1837, he launched a rebellion against *bakufu* troops in Osaka on behalf of famine-stricken farmers in the area. His summons (*gekibun*) was for sustained revolt against a hopelessly evil *bakufu*. In tactical terms, the rebellion failed, despite destruction by fire of one-fourth of Osaka. Yet, like his less-volatile predecessors Nakae and Kumazawa, Ōshio became a cultural hero. Farmers in the Osaka area revered him, and activists in the 1850s saw him as a crucial spiritual "model" for total and active rejection of the *bakufu*.

Perhaps of greater importance, Ōshio's conception of action became "nationalized." Ethical "ideal" meshed with concrete national history and, especially, with the rhetoric, metaphors, and political imagery that make up a belief in a continuing cultural history. Ōshio's slogan of "saving the people" (*kyūmin*), with slight reworking, became "protecting the country" (*jōi*, or, literally, "expelling the foreigners"). Ōshio's idealism, then, took on its fullest significance as it was generalized into a concept of action for national survival. While this possibility was present in Ōshio, it was given explicit content and focus by "national studies," which developed concurrently with Ōyōmei idealism.

Like Ōyōmei thought, national studies was idealistic and basically "nonbureaucratic" in conceptual content. It defined society in terms of an "ideal spirit" that evolved in a distinctive manner in history. Like Ōyōmei, its view of action rested on intuition and not on bureaucratic reason. It demanded faith and loyal commitment over observation and rational calculation. Concerned primarily with explaining cultural distinctiveness, national studies meshed with late Tokugawa activism, infusing nationalistic content into abstract ethical norms.

The pivotal figure in national studies was Motoori Norinaga (1730–1801).[8] A brilliant and complex thinker, Motoori drew on two previous strands of thought and used the combination to affirm unequivocally the uniqueness of Japanese culture. Drawing on the work of the little-known scholar Keichū (1640–1701), Motoori developed a theory of aethetics that viewed Japanese literature as the elegant expression of the pure human feelings of a past age and not as documents of moral didactics. The *Manyōshū, Tale of Genji*, and other Japanese classics, he insisted, should be viewed through such an aesthetic perspective.

Motoori also drew from the secular historicism of Ogyū Sorai. Although a sinophile who was outspoken in his contempt for Japanese culture, Ogyū developed a view of history that could be applied readily to explain the distinctiveness of Japan. Culture and ethics, Ogyū had said, were historical creations, not metaphysical necessities. Societies therefore had an explicit beginning in an ancient world and they evolved divergent patterns of discourse over time. Motoori extracted the principle of historical relativity (primarily through his mentor Kamo Mabuchi, 1697–1769) and applied it to Japanese cultural history.

At its inception, Motoori reasoned, Japanese society was joined together by a common human feeling. So spontaneous was this feeling that it appeared to be of nature itself, pure and devoid of ethical convolutions. It was also passionate, irrepressible, and as inevitable as love and hate, happiness and sadness, fear of pain and awe of the mysterious. The uniqueness of Japan, Motoori concluded, lay in its acceptance of these human emotions and its striving to express their beauty in creative and elegant language.

[8] Shigeru Matsumoto, *Motoori Norinaga, 1730–1801* (Cambridge: Harvard University Press, 1970). Some of Motoori's writings are presented in reasonably readable modern Japanese in Ishikawa Jun, ed., *Nihon no meicho*, vol. 21, *Motoori Norinaga* (Tokyo: Chūōkōronsha, 1970). An excellent discussion on the development of national studies is Matsumoto Sannosuke, *Tennōseikokka to seijishisō*, pp. 9–61. The essay first appeared as "Kokugaku no seiritsu" in *Iwanami kōza, Nihon rekishi*, vol. 10, pp. 155–98. Also informative are Haga Noboru, *Bakumatsu kokugaku no tenkai* (Tokyo: Hanawa shobō, 1963); and Itō Tasaburō, "Edo jidai kōki no rekishi shisō," in *Rekishi shisō no tenkai*, pp. 213–42.

Motoori's aesthetic theory seems far removed from political development. And, indeed, one of his lasting influences is precisely the view that creativity springs from the personal spirit, utterly without regard to politics. Yet, there is political complexity in Motoori, for while artistic creativity is personal, art, itself, can be used for political ends. There is logical consistency in this view: Culture once created becomes "natural," part of the "fixed" environment; it is man's "fate" to be born into culture. And although art is not a bureaucratic fabrication, it is vital for the maintenance of the cultural order. Remaining within Ogyū's conceptual framework, Motoori subordinated art to political need. This view easily led to an ideological beautification of the monarchy to assure domestic tranquility, and, also, to a criticism of political ineffectualness, institutional failings, and human miseries, due to the *bakufu's* cultural insensitivity.

Motoori's primary importance, however, is not his political criticism, but his religious perception of Japanese primitivism. While Ogyū concerned himself with explaining the rationality of structures, Motoori sought to uncover the spirituality of the Japanese personality. In a pure and simple world, unencumbered by artificial thoughts of hell, transmigration, ritual mourning, and filial piety, Motoori sought a culture of "pure feeling (*magokoro*) that connected Japan's origin with the elegant and metaphorical literature of later times. His historical logic was sound: The cultural present, traced backward over time leads through interconnected precedents to a mythic past. His method was likewise sound: Philological techniques applied to ancient Japanese language (as he did with monumental erudition on the *Kojiki*) can tell a great deal about the spiritual life of the ancients. His central quest, however, was religious, to discover a continuous native faith. Antiquity was not to be judged but believed in and accepted as an aesthetic reality.

It was this religious dimension that gave political meaning to Motoori's aesthetics. Antiquity was not of the past; it was inseparable from the whole of subsequent history. Faith in the ancients meant faith in a divine continuity of the Japanese. Ancient gods (*kami*) were gods in the present and the monarch was descended from the greatest deity of antiquity, the sun goddess, Amaterasu. The monarch stood beyond conventional judgment as a cultural absolute, as the sun in the sky, as the total manifestation of the mystery and essential feeling of antiquity in a continuing historical present. And like mythic antiquity, history was beautiful for its mystery. Like literature, it could not be perceived with conceptions of ethics and virtue. It was the makings of gods who are neither divine because of their virtue nor necessarily virtuous because they are divine. The history they made, therefore, was beyond conventional reason and modes of control. Like creators of great art, the makers of history were extraordinary: The creative political sage of Ogyū was, for Motoori, possessed by divine spirit.

Although not an iconoclast, Motoori had gone far toward rationalizing action based on a national faith—action for the national cultural essence, however that might be defined. This principle of activism was singled out for exclusive emphasis by Motoori's followers, notably Hirata Atsutane (1776–1843).[9] For Hirata, the study of aesthetics and emotional elegance was "nonscholarship" (*mugaku*). True commitment meant to act in accordance with faith in the superiority of national culture. The superiority of Shintoism over all other forms of religions was a matter of faith, not of documentation and scholarly debate. All societies ought to believe in themselves as a spiritual community; yet, such a self-confirming faith had been denied the Japanese people through bureaucratic oppression, corruption, and, worst of all, blind adulation of Chinese and Buddhist ideas. With Hirata, national studies turned into an angry call for action in the present. The monarchy became more than an aesthetic symbol and a religious embodiment of antiquity: It was an ideal of a just spiritual paradisium that ought to be "restored."

In its religious character national studies provided an intui-

---

[9] Matsumoto, *Tennōseikokka*, pp. 50–61. A readable biography is Tahara Tsuguo, *Hirata Atsutane* (Tokyo: Yoshikawa kōbunkan, 1963). See also Haga Noboru and Matsumoto Sannosuke, eds., *Nihon shisō taikei*, vol. 15, *Kokugaku undō no shisō* (Tokyo: Iwanami shoten, 1971).

tional basis for action akin to Ōyōmei idealism. Action taken decisively against the present was understood as a drastic departure from the normative assumptions of existing politics and ideology. Both Ōyōmei idealism and national studies emphasized a true commitment to act based on faith not on rational explication. Both legitimated radical action with references to ideals outside the present. Ōyōmei idealism, which had a cosmic conception of truth, and national studies, which rejected universal truths in favor of an indigenous antiquity, converged as theories of action. Ōshio Heihachirō and Hirata Atsutane stood on common ground. Both went beyond the ordinary constraints of Tokugawa feudalism and were indeed defiant of it. Neither had a structured vision of the future, since this was extraneous to their idealistic convictions. But both were legitimating models for iconoclastic action generated within the Tokugawa *baku-han* order, an order that managed itself throughout much of its history with impressive bureaucratic discipline.

LOYALISM AS REBELLION

In the 1850s and 1860s, rebellious action punctuated the political process with astonishing regularity. This is not to suggest the rise of an organized revolt. But previous patterns of predictable bureaucratic relations were drastically disrupted, creating political turmoil and intellectual uncertainty. The idealized goal of Ōshio, Hirata, and their followers to "save the people" suddenly was refocused to mean defending the entire country and its true historical essence. National defense, "expelling the barbarians" (*jōi*) as this was colorfully called, was now raised to an equivalent normative status with true loyalism or "loyalty to the emperor" (*sonnō*), which everyone accepted as an unassailable ethical *princip*. Linked together into a single compound, *sonnō-jōi* legitimated the rejection, either through a verbal demand for structural change or through violent action, of the political status quo as represented by the *bakufu*.

Men from Mito were again active. Nariaki himself, released

from house exile in 1853, involved himself in criticism and intrigue, disputing the *bakufu's* choice of a shogunal successor by sponsoring a "loyalist" candidate, and generally urging a new conciliar structure (*kōbugattai*) to allow men in the court and regional leaders to participate in forming national policy. But besides men from Mito there were others involved in vigorous criticism and rebellious intrigue.

A conspicuously visible group, called the "loyalist faction" (*kinnō ha*), emerged on the political scene.[10] Joined together more by a sense of spiritual commitment than by organization, these "loyalists" came from all parts of the country. Many consciously severed ties with their fief and became masterless *samurai*, or *rōnin*. In contrast to the idealized medieval *rōnin* who retired out of sadness to literature or religion, these loyalist *rōnin* were of a different sort. While retaining sword and status, they were defiantly proud of their autonomy; and they cherished their distance from bureaucratic details and ceremonial duties, and projected a self-assured yet somewhat relaxed image in dress and social manners. They remain etched as heroic types in the mind of modern Japan. Opportunists and adventurers at their worst, they were also idealists and literate radicals. In the literature of the period and in historical accounts, therefore, they are often described as *shishi*, activists with true inner convictions.

Many of the loyalists went to Edo to study Ōyōmei idealism with Satō Issai and practical philosophy from Sakuma Shōzan (1811–64), both important intellectuals serving the *bakufu*. Others sought discourse with Aizawa and Fujita Tōko in Mito. Still others went to Nagasaki to study Dutch, and then English, so that they could grapple with the barbarians on their own terms. A few actually hoped to visit the West. Some, such as Sakamoto

---

[10] The development of the Tokugawa loyalists and their ethic of action is discussed in Sagara, *Kinsei no jukyo shisō*, pp. 207–35; and Matsumoto, *Tennōseikokka*, pp. 62–117. Two stimulating paperbacks that deal with this subject are Ichii Saburō, *Meiji Ishin no tetsugaku* (Tokyo: Kōdansha, 1967); and Sugiura Mimpei, *Ishin zen'ya no bungaku* (Tokyo: Iwanami shoten, 1967).

Ryōma (1835–67) of Tosa, relied on political persuasion and maneuver, forging ties with men in the court and loyalist leaders from Mito and Aizu. Others appear to have been anarchists. Takeichi Zuizan (1829–65) from Tosa, plotted terrorism, believing this to be a necessary stage in the birth of a new order. Maki Izumi (1813–64) son of a Shinto priest, who bore a striking resemblance to Hirata Atsutane, likewise was committed to violent rebellion.

Rising above all the loyalists was Yoshida Shōin (1830–59) of Chōshū, perhaps the greatest single inspiration to activists in this period.[11] In search for a true theory of action he traveled to Edo to study with idealists. He read Yamagata Daini's denunciation of the *bakufu* and incorporated this view into a rejection of his political world. For Yoshida, Ōshio Heihachirō represented the outer limit of protest, and he pondered what lay beyond it in strategy. Like Ōshio, he reconsidered the importance of the late Ming loyalists who fought the Manchus in the early seventeenth century and read deeply in their political idealism. Yoshida embodied many of the characteristics of the ideal *shishi* or committed activist: acceptance of the ethic of total self-dedication, a view of the present and the immediate past as irredeemably evil, a belief in a cultural essence that ought to be "restored" to strengthen the country, an uncompromising view of existing bureaucratic "reason" as deceptive and ineffectual against the threat of Western power, and finally, an understanding that previously sanctioned guidelines to loyal action were no longer trustworthy.

Most of the loyalists were surprisingly young men. Yoshida, Sakamoto, Kusaga Genzui (1840–64), Takasugi Shinsaku (1839–67), Kido Kōin (1833–77), Fujita Koshirō (1842–65), Hirano Kuniomi (1828–64), Hashimoto Sanai (1828–64), and Saigō

11 See Harootunian, *Toward Restoration*, and also Matsumoto, *Tennōseikokka*, pp. 94–108. On Yoshida's students, see Naramoto Tatsuya and Matsuura Rei, "Shōka sonjuku no hitobito," in Konishi Shirō, ed., *Nihon jimbutsushi taikei*, vol. 5, *Kindai*, 1 (Tokyo: Asakura shoten, 1960), pp. 39–64. Naramoto Tatsuya has also written a biography, *Yoshida Shōin* (Tokyo: Iwanami shoten, 1961). A well-known biography from the prewar period is Tokutomi Iichirō, *Yoshida Shōin* (Tokyo: Min'yūsha, 1908).

Takamori (1827–77) were men in their mid-twenties and early thirties. Many were to be killed in battle or executed in the tumultuous events of the 1860s. Yet their mark on late Tokugawa political history is indelible. As individuals and in small groups, they converged on Kyoto in the 1850s and 1860s. There, where the emperor resided in exile, they engaged each other in angry discussion about the outrageous political situation and debated endlessly, in obscure inns and *sake* houses, on the proper strategy for action. Sometimes they fought each other in violent encounters (such as at Teradaya in Kyoto in 1862), struggling over whether to redistribute power within a reorganized *bakufu* or to confront the *bakufu* with direct military rebellion. Above all, whether as "moderates" or "radicals," they made it exceedingly difficult for the *bakufu* to adapt structures in terms of the previous allocation of power. No longer could the *bakufu* unilaterally impose a policy of national importance without facing a wide range of demands, including the redistribution of political responsibility.

The precariousness of the *bakufu*'s position can be seen in the events of the 1850s. Confronted with Perry's ultimatum in the fall of 1853, the *bakufu* in circuitous language appealed for baronial consensus confirming the practicality of ending seclusionism and opening the country. The *daimyō* responded with more than loyal support but with substantive political advice as well. As participants in deciding policy, a good many advised the *bakufu* to keep the country closed and to formulate at once a comprehensive defense strategy. Faced with some ambivalence among the *daimyō*, the *bakufu* turned to the emperor, only to receive grudging approval and a stiff reminder of the *bakufu*'s primary responsibility of keeping the country autonomous.

From this point on, due to developments within the country, the *bakufu* was not allowed to stabilize itself as a political system. The Mito critique once again focused itself on the *bakufu* to show concretely its ineffectualness in a national crisis. With more telling effect than in the 1830s, the point was again made that the *bakufu* alone was not equipped to handle problems that were national in scope. Loyal *daimyō* and members of the court, previously excluded from decision making, should be fully incorporated in a new "council" under the legitimating aegis of the emperor. Besides Mito Nariaki, *daimyō* from Echizen, Satsuma, and Chōshū argued in this vein, as did court loyalists Sanjō Saneomi (1837–91) and Iwakura Tomomi (1825–83), and lower-level loyalists, such as Sakamoto Ryōma and Hashimoto Sanai.[12] The issue, clearly, was not so much whether "unequal treaties" should be signed, but how decisions of this kind should be arrived at.

Against mounting criticism, the *bakufu* chose not to redefine its political structure from within. Although appearing on occasion to be receptive to a conciliar mode of governance, it chose to open the country and sign unequal treaties on its own responsibility, without regard to the wishes of the emperor, his court, and loyalist activists in Kyoto. Under its senior chief councillor, Ii Naosuke (1815–60), the *bakufu* turned its power against the loyalists. In the famous Ansei Purge of 1858–59, Ii Naosuke declared Mito Nariaki *persona non grata* in *bakufu* affairs and again ordered him and his advisers into house exile. Three other *daimyō* friends of Nariaki were also exiled. Twelve well-known loyalists in Kyoto were hunted down and executed. Yoshida Shōin, Hashimoto Sanai, and Umeda Umpin (1815–59) were martyred at this time. In all, some one hundred loyalists were arrested before the purge was over.[13]

[12] Many of these personalities have not been treated in Western monographs. A well known study is Marius B. Jansen, *Sakamoto Ryōma and the Meiji Restoration* (Princeton: Princeton University Press, 1961). George M. Wilson has written "The Bakumatsu Intellectual in Action: Hashimoto Sanai in the Political Crisis of 1858," in Craig and Shively, eds., *Personality in Japanese History*, pp. 234–63. The studies of Harootunian and Matsumoto mentioned in the previous note also add a great deal. Two interesting books are Naramoto Tatsuya, ed., *Ishin no shishi* (Tokyo: Chikuma shobō, 1967); and, on the daily life of the loyalists, Haga Noboru, *Bakumatsu shishi no seikatsu* (Tokyo: Yūzankaku, 1970).

[13] The political details are discussed in concise form by W. G. Beasley, *Select Documents of Japanese Foreign Policy, 1853–1868* (London: Oxford University Press, 1955), pp. 1–93; and more recently in his *The Meiji Restora-*

With the Ansei Purge, violence became part of the political process. On the morning of March 3, 1860, outside of the Sakurada gate of the *bakufu*'s castle in Edo, eighteen loyalists from Mito and Echizen assaulted Ii Naosuke, the highest bureaucratic official in the *bakufu* and assassinated him. This unprecedented act staggered the *bakufu*. Ii's successor (Andō Nobumasa 1819–71) retreated to a conciliatory position, seeking support from the leaders of Satsuma and Echizen, but he too was physically assaulted (January 5, 1862), again by loyalist swordsmen from Mito, and forced into premature retirement. In the early 1860s (known as Bunkyū), violence repeatedly undermined the *bakufu*'s political credibility.

Mito loyalists attacked Rutherford Alcock, the ambassador from England, and killed two of his aides, forcing the *bakufu* to pay for the reparations. Men from Satsuma killed two Englishmen and fought the invading British to a standstill, forcing the British to again collect reparations from the *bakufu*. Chōshū loyalists, led by Kusaka Genzui and Takasugi Shinsaku, attacked and burned the British consulate being constructed outside of Edo. Later these same Chōshū loyalists fired on foreign ships off of Shimonoseki and engaged the Westerners in battle. Soundly beaten by Western guns, Chōshū nonetheless refused to pay reparations, a staggering 3 million, which the *bakufu* in the end was compelled to honor. In Kyoto, about seventy loyalists from fifteen *han*, including Tosa Okayama, and Mikawa, known as the "band embodying Heaven's will" (*Tenchūgumi*), attacked *bakufu* troops. In Fukuoka, the loyalist Hirano Kuniomi raised an army including some 2,000 farmers and launched a rebellion. In Mito, Fujita Koshirō (a son of Fujita Tōko) threw that do-

---

tion (London: Oxford University Press, 1972). See also George B. Sansom, *The Western World and Japan* (New York: Alfred A. Knopf, 1958), pp. 275–309. Good coverage of many of the events are found in Shigakkai, ed., *Meiji Ishin shi kenkyū* (Tokyo: Fuzambō, 1929); Oka Yoshitake, *Kindai Nihon no keisei* (Tokyo: Kōbundō, 1947); and Yanaihara Tadao, *Gendai Nihon shōshi*, 2 vols. (Tokyo: Misuzu shobō, 1952). Also of interest is Naramato Tatsuya, "Yūhan no taitō," *Iwanami kōza, Nihon rekishi*, vol. 13, pp. 251–88.

main into a state of civil war. Of greater significance, in what is known as the Incident at the Forbidden Gate (Kimmon no hen), loyalists from Chōshū, led by Kusaka Genzui and Maki Izumi, attacked bakufu troops in Kyoto in an effort to capture that city. It was this incident, seen as a culmination of all of the acts of violent defiance, that prompted the bakufu to commit its military power to halt all further internal rebellion.

In late summer 1864, the bakufu launched the first of two invasions of Chōshū. Whether or not this "chastisement" was justified is moot. The price for departing from tradition and militarily intervening in the internal affairs of a han was exceedingly high. Within Chōshū, three loyalist ministers of the highest level (known as san-karō) were executed to save the han from the wrath of the bakufu. This immediately defined the loyalists of Chōshū as rebels against their han, and civil war became inevitable in Chōshū. Within a year, the loyalist rebels rallying around Takasugi, Kido Kōin, Maebara Issei (1834–76), and others, using modern guns and a multiclass army, seized power in Chōshū. Then, with a firm military alliance with Satsuma (arranged by Sakamoto Ryōma), Chōshū turned as a baronial domain, but in the cause of national unification, to challenge the Tokugawa bakufu. In the bakufu's second invasion of Chōshū (September 21, 1866), the superiority of the loyalist army was established with astonishing speed, irreparably destroying the bakufu's claim to paramount power in the land.[14]

---

[14] The point of departure in reading on the Meiji Restoration is E. Herbert Norman, Japan's Emergence as a Modern State (New York: Institute of Pacific Relations, 1940; reprinted, 1960). Two provocative analyses are Albert M. Craig, Chōshū in the Meiji Restoration (Cambridge: Harvard University Press, 1961); and Harootunian, Toward Restoration. Recent additions are Beasley, The Meiji Restoration; and Paul Akamatsu, Meiji 1868: Revolution and Counter-Revolution in Japan (Evanston: Harper and Row, Publishers, 1972; first published in French as Meiji 1868: Révolution et contrerévolution au Japon, Paris, 1968). An indispensable guide in Japanese is Rekishigaku kenkyūkai, ed., Meiji ishin shi kōza, 6 vols. (Tokyo: Heibonsha, 1958). Other important works in Japanese include: Hani Gorō, Meiji Ishin (Tokyo: Iwanami shoten, 1946), and his Meiji Ishin shi kenkyū (Tokyo: Iwanami shoten, 1956); Naramoto Tatsuya, Ishin shi no kadai (Tokyo: Hakutō shokan, 1949);

The reverberations of these acts of political violence were felt throughout the country. Once certain of its actions within established political confines, the *samurai* class, in particular, found itself deeply divided and torn by the uncertainties caused by conflicting definitions of loyalty. No longer did "loyalty" necessarily mean the suppression of "rebellion"; loyalty could mean rebellion itself. And no longer was this view of loyalty merely an abstract possibility or an isolated incident on the fringes of political society, but a mode of action regularly and dramatically acted out, with utter conviction and commitment, by intelligent young men in the most visible political arenas of Edo, Kyoto, Chōshū, and Mito. Indeed, in every *han* the issue of loyalty as support of, or rebellion against, the existing order was debated with intense acrimony and, quite often, violence. Thus, while the *han* remained firm as a political boundary, preventing indiscriminate and diffuse spillage of violence and plunder from one region to the next, the political impact of internal rebellion in the Bunkyū years of the early 1860s was profound and deep. In the end, each "house" maintained its own order and projected a semblance of outward unity while displaying a conspicuous absence of baronial rally in support of the faltering *bakufu*. There was, instead, an uneasy and ambivalent inaction.

Perhaps most significant, rebellion in the cause of a wider loyalty acted as a decisive catalyst in the political development of the 1860s. It erased as an intellectual issue the theoretical legitimacy of revolt. Requiring no further conceptual justification, rebellion became a practical matter of strategy. In short, for internal enemies of the *bakufu*, whatever their motivation, the political issue of the day had shifted from "whether" to "how" to launch criticism against the *bakufu*. Then, as the *bakufu* appeared increasingly indefensible as a political system, the concern over critical strategy shifted to the level of "what" the newly "restored" order should be. Victors, vanquished, and the unde-

Inoue Kiyoshi, *Nihon gendaishi*, vol. 1, *Meiji Ishin* (Tokyo: Tokyo daigaku shuppankai, 1951); and Tōyama Shigeki, *Meiji Ishin* (Tokyo: Iwanami shoten, 1951).

cided (for few were indifferent) all were aware of the decisive evolution of late Tokugawa politics.

There emerged out of this rapid chain of events a political vision of Japan's future. Restorationism as rebellion against the *bakufu* rendered history irreversible: A return to the immediate past, or to a point where the *bakufu* was at its splendor was no longer tenable. The restored monarchy, however, did not have a bureaucracy with which to rule. Out of the growing realization that a totally new order must be designed there surfaced several pressing political questions: How might loyalism as rebellion be restructured to render further rebellion treasonous; how might society best be mobilized to meet the Western threat; and can a set of structures be devised that might last into the future as a creative achievement of restorationism?

These questions spoke to the unmistakable resurgence of a utilitarian discourse about politics that had been cultivated within the *baku-han* order itself. Firmly fixed in that bureaucratic ideology was the iconoclastic view that bureaucratic institutions must be responsive to the pressures of history. Not metaphysically sacrosanct, political structures were redesigned in continuing time. In general, structures were either decentralized (*hōken*, or "feudal") or centralized (*gun-ken*), as in imperial China. But in either case, structures were held together by rationally contrived norms that were assumed to be "fixed." Having rejected the decentralized pattern of recent political history, the logical alternative for the future appeared to be centralized rule under the monarchy. There was no delusion, however, that such a system must be "Chinese" in design. There was the added understanding, however naïvely conceived, that the restoration of loyalty under imperial rule must involve a drastic departure from previous history and that the monarchical symbol must be identified unequivocally with a new future.

The desire to look for new political structures was embedded in the utilitarian component of restorationism. Traceable to functional and eclectic bureaucratic ideology as described in the previous chapter, it was also woven into the articulations of the Mito school in the early nineteenth century. Its importance as political ideology inevitably returned as the fall of the *bakufu* became imminent, for in this view, bureaucratic constructs were essential to social existence. This resurgence of a utilitarian perspective, however, created deep feelings of ambivalence and, in the end, political conflict among the loyalists. Sharp differences emerged once the *bakufu* was defeated regarding the proper future course of the restoration; and these differences were directly identifiable with the two halves of restorationism, utilitarian bureaucratic thought and idealistic action. It was the utilitarian perspective that emerged triumphant in the construction of modern Japan, while the idealism in restorationism would express itself first in revolt against the new bureaucratism and then in taking on new intellectual content and modes of action, persisting as an important intellectual option against modern forms of bureaucratic rule.

4

The Meiji Quest for Constitutional and Ideological Certitude

The Emperor Meiji was only sixteen when "restored" to power in 1868. In Tokyo, the "eastern capital" (previously called Edo), he was enthroned in the former *shōgun's* castle, symbol of *bakufu* power for well over two hundred years. An exuberant youth, he was subjected to intense and sometimes stern training by his loyalist aides, who, in his name, launched the revolutionary transformation in politics and industry that came to be called "the splendor of Meiji." Primarily from the territorial domains of Satsuma and Chōshū, these loyalists began the Meiji era in the spring of 1868 with a pledge, the Imperial Charter Oath, to dissolve the Tokugawa feudal order. They put down internal rebellions against them, the most serious coming from Saigō Takamori, a leader of the Meiji Restoration itself, and began the sustained search for a stable bureaucratic order held together by new organizing principles or "fixed norms"—*kempō*—"constitution," as such a set of norms now came to be called. Their aim was to end arbitrary government and stimulate new forms of constructive, loyal action.

Parallel to this search for new structures, political ideologies, many from current Western thought, were studied and adapted for Japan's entrance into its modern era. While theoretically diverse, all of the new modes of thought were consciously contrasted with previous feudal ideology, but, at the same time, were used to stress the continuing need for social commitment despite bewildering historical disruption and change. In justifying change they provided credible conceptual underpinnings to a wide variety of action deemphasized in previous ethical thought; they supported the "constitutional" reorganization of the country; and, despite an initial rejection of history, they gave theoretical support to the selective use of the past for modern ends. The construction of new institutions and the accompanying fresh formulations of political thought were not a harmonious process, but together they define Meiji Japan's political experience.

The Triumph of Political Pragmatism

The political settlement following the Restoration was characterized by great tension and turmoil, resulting from a struggle between rival forces strongly committed to different modes of achieving national greatness. It is a history, however, that unequivocally demonstrates the triumph of pragmatic thought and action embedded in late Tokugawa restorationism itself. This is plainly evident in the revolutionary dissolution of the Tokugawa feudal order and the steady consolidation of oligarchic leadership in the hands of Ōkubo Toshimichi (1830–78) and Kido Kōin in the 1870s and Itō Hirobumi (1841–1909), Yamagata Aritomo (1838–1922), and a handful of other men—often referred to as the Meiji Genrō—in the 1880s.

These men were mainly from Satsuma and Chōshū, but more important than their common geographical origin was their shared understanding that the Restoration was a mandate to create, through bureaucratic means, a powerful, wealthy, and autonomous Japanese nation. Former enemies such as Katsu Kaishū (1823–99) who served the *bakufu,* and commoners such as Shibuzawa Eiichi (1840–1931), who shared their view, received positions of great responsibility in the new government, as in planning a modern navy and a banking system with which Katsu and Shibuzawa were involved respectively. Other loyalist leaders such as Saigō Takamori, Etō Shimpei (1834–74), and Maebara Issei, who had agreed on the ultimate end but resisted the "bureaucratic" approach on emotional and idealistic grounds, were eventually expelled from the oligarchic center even though they had been important comrades in the rebellion against the *bakufu*.

Uniting to dismantle the *bakufu* initially had created a bond among the loyalists. They served notice of the Restoration's drastic departure from the previous system of *bakufu* politics in the form of the Imperial Charter Oath. Although the details of the new order were withheld and the rhetoric (drafted primarily by Kido and then endorsed by all the others) was traditional and exceedingly cryptic, the iconoclastic intent was unmistakable.[1]

To rectify the *bakufu*'s previous refusal to share power with baronial leaders and their ministers in the regions, the document began with a pledge to share power. "All affairs of the state," it read, "shall be determined by public discussion." It was a concise restatement of the Mito critique, well known since the 1830s, that loyal leaders of the nation should be included in establishing policy for the entire nation. Important structural implications were embedded in this critique, as in the argument for a *daimyō* council, but there was no hint of parliamentary democracy in its vocabulary, although a promise of representative government was gradually read into the oath.

In incisive and terse language the oath further pledged pervasive social reorganization that would unify aristocrats and commoners, administrators and subjects. Previous functional and hereditary classes would be eradicated, allowing everyone to freely move, buy, sell, educate himself, and choose an occupation without regard to previous status and geographical location. It was a pledge to select new talent without regard to the past.

---

[1] A translation of the Imperial Charter Oath is found in Tsunoda, de Bary, and Keene, eds., *Sources of the Japanese Tradition*, p. 644; and in Sansom, *The Western World and Japan*, p. 318.

Finally, there was the admission in the oath that previous conventions and ideology would no longer be relied upon uncritically as guidelines for action. A firm plea was made to discard all anachronistic customs and to look throughout the world for new knowledge—a declaration, in effect, of the loyalists' commitment to separate Japan not only from a good part of its own history but from the Asian cultural zone in general.

A number of precarious and calculated risks were suggested in the oath. The agreement to share power was included to lure support from skeptical barons and remnants of *bakufu* supporters who might choose civil war, not as a concession to establish deliberative assemblies. The promise of social mobility was not expected to result in massive defection from the countryside, but, indeed, to foster continued intensive work on the land by allowing former peasants to own property. The plea to destroy anachronistic customs, it was assumed, would not involve the monarchy, which, since ancient times, was symbolic of a continuous social history and would now stand unequivocally for a new future. In a similar manner, the encouragement to seek new knowledge was given with the understanding that loyal identification with the Japanese nation would remain unassailably firm. This was in accordance with a formula stated by leading late Tokugawa intellectuals, notably Sakuma Shōzan, that cultural essence was particular to national history, while science, the study of natural principles, was universal and therefore everywhere applicable regardless of the specific character of a cultural experience.

The guidelines of the oath were quickly followed between 1869 and 1875. *Han* domains were abolished, ending the principle of semiautonomy favored by the *bakufu*. Since *bakufu* hegemony had been destroyed, its "charters" guaranteeing the two hundred fifty *daimyō* their lordship over various *han* were no longer legally or ethically binding. In polite yet firm language the *daimyō* were advised to return their "charters" to the ultimate *de jure* source, the emperor. Then, in various agglomerations, domains were redefined as "prefectures," numbering about fifty, within a proposed but not yet finalized central system. No *daimyō* was given a new charter, although some, who represented the interests and needs of the central regime, were designated "governors" of the new prefectures.

Without the *han* as an intermediate construct, the entire country was declared an indivisible public domain under the aegis of the imperial house. Legal ownership of land, once held by privileged barons, was drastically transferred downward to the local village level without fear of subinfeudation. Moreover, surplus agricultural wealth once controlled and dispersed by the *daimyō* among his *samurai* retainers in the form of stipends was also transferred downward to the local farming households and taxed in the form of a comprehensive land tax. It was, of course, this new fiscal structure that provided the capital for the industrial revolution of the 1880s.

The dissolution of the *daimyō* and their *han* led quickly to the declassing of the *samurai*. Without properly chartered lords, the close to three million *samurai* were suddenly rendered "masterless." To ease the sudden shock of declassment, the term *shizoku*, or "former *samurai*," was used to maintain something of the social dignity of the Tokugawa aristocracy. As a practical matter, however, the *samurai* were precipitously declassed. Their hereditary stipends were terminated and, instead, they were given bonds with a fixed value that drastically declined in the economic confusion and resulting inflation of the 1870s. Beyond this, they were denied their conspicuous symbols of class identification and were ordered to shed their topknot hairstyle and, more crucially, their powerful swords. They were then instructed to turn their considerable talents to commercial enterprise (long held by the *samurai* as an insulting occupation) to promote the national cause of accumulating wealth and strength. Virtually over night, untold tens of thousands of former *samurai* sank into a state of penury as they failed to compete effectively with shrewd merchants and peasants and awkwardly squandered their bonds on poorly conceived economic ventures. Legally, as already noted, the regime reinforced this declassment by guaranteeing commoners the right to own property, invest, and accumulate profit, giving many the opportunity to rise from lowly levels to great prominence as industrialists. Moreover, the government endorsed universal education and universal military conscription. In short, inside of several short years, the *samurai* were deprived of their monopoly over arms, knowledge, and surplus agricultural wealth, the key substantive items that had defined them as a proud aristocracy; and they were compelled to compete with commoners who exhibited an unusual burst of entrepreneurial energy throughout the nation.[2]

At first glance, the declassing of an aristocracy by other members of that very same class appears to be something of a historical anomaly. Yet, as previously emphasized, this iconoclasm, especially as espoused by Ōkubo and Kido, was woven into the intellectual fabric of late Tokugawa restorationist thought. The view that the *bakufu* was unacceptable because it was ineffectual sharply brought into focus, with the defeat of the *bakufu*, the need to refashion the political and social order to deal concretely with the Western threat. Of the highest priority in this view was the construction of a new legal system far more comprehensive and effective than the one provided by the *bakufu*. It was essential to mobilize the talent and wealth of the entire country, and the declassing of the *samurai*, however painful, was entirely consistent with this utilitarian view of politics.

The sudden declassment of the *samurai*, however, triggered a severe crisis in the Meiji leadership. It was an issue that exposed the opposing principles to which individual loyalists were intellectually committed, a matter concealed previously by the politics of rebellion. Loyalist leaders such as Saigō Takamori, Maebara Issei, Etō Shimpei, and Itagaki Taisuke believed the policy of declassment to be excessively harsh and threatening to the "spirit

---

[2] Good descriptions of the dissolution of the old order are Haraguchi Kiyoshi, "Bakuhan taisei no kaitai," *Iwanami kōza, Nihon rekishi*, vol. 15, *Kindai*, 2 (Tokyo: Iwanami shoten, 1962), pp. 1–52; and Masumi Junnosuke, *Nihon seitōshi ron*, 4 vols. (Tokyo: Tokyo daigaku shuppankai, 1965), vol. 1, pp. 1–114. In English, see Harry D. Harootunian, "The Economic Rehabilitation of the Samurai in the Early Meiji Period," *The Journal of Asian Studies* 19, no. 4 (1960): 433–44.

of the Restoration." These men approved the dissolution of the *bakufu* order and the mobilization of talent throughout the country and held firmly to the view that the Restoration was an achievement of human spirit which ought now to unify the nation in a rally against the Western threat. Thus Saigō, the focal personality of this position, supported universal conscription and the dissolution of *bakufu* structures, but he objected strenuously to the undignified bureaucratic assault on the *samurai* as unjustifiably harsh and foreign to the goals of restorationism and fatal to the spirit of revolutionary activism that had made the rebellion against the *bakufu* possible in the first place.[3]

Beginning as early as 1870, distrust and hostility began to appear among the loyalists in power. Maebara Issei left the government in opposition to the dissolution of the loyalist army of Chōshū. A student of Yoshida Shōin and a close comrade of Kido, Maebara had been instrumental in shaping the multiclass army of Chōshū that had defeated the *bakufu*'s army. While Kido, Ōkubo, Yamagata, and others saw a regional Chōshū army as a contradiction to the goals of centralization and universal conscription, Maebara strongly believed that the army stood for a precious élan that was vital to national strength. The dispute persisted through the early 1870s and then flared into the open in the fall of 1873 when the new regime debated whether it should involve itself in a military chastisement of Korea for its insulting treatment of Japanese envoys. Ōkubo and Kido prevailed against such action as indefensible in the light of more pressing needs, forcing those who supported such a course of action to resign from the government. Saigō, Etō Shimpei, Itagaki Taisuke (1837–1919), Gotō Shōjirō (1838–97), and some fifty or so allies left the government at this time. Saigō and Etō returned

---

[3] Much has been written on Saigō, although many of the works are not scholarly efforts. Yoshida Tsunekichi has written a short piece, "Saigō Takamori," in Konishi, ed., *Nihon jimbutsushi taikei*, vol. 5, pp. 92–122. Other recent works include Kimura Ki, *Saigō Nanshū* (Tokyo: Sekka sha, 1966); Ikenami Shōtarō, *Saigō Takamori* (Tokyo: Jimbutsu ōrai sha, 1967); and Haga Noboru, *Saigō Takamori* (Tokyo: Yūzankaku, 1968). A fine recent addition is Inoue Kiyoshi, *Saigō Takamori*, 2 vols. (Tokyo: Chuōkoronsha, 1970).

to their regional homes (Satsuma and Hizen respectively) to teach *samurai* malcontents and, eventually along with Maebara, to revolt against the Meiji government. Itagaki and Gotō organized struggling *samurai* of Tosa into a "self-help society" (*Risshisha*), which grew and gained in sophistication to spearhead a regionally based movement of protest called the popular-rights movement (*jiyūminken undō*). In 1881 this group reorganized itself into the Freedom Party (*Jiyūtō*), which continued to be, despite changes in names and internal realignments, one of the two major political parties in the Japanese constitutional order.[4]

What needs to be emphasized is that the road to rebellion taken by Saigō and that to party politics taken by Itagaki, although apparently contrasting, were actually interlinked by a common intellectual emphasis on the importance of an essential spiritual dignity in loyalism, which should be supported rather than attacked insensitively by bureaucratic means. Saigō, relying on traditional rhetoric and imagery, characterized this fundamental spiritual power as "respect for heaven and love of the people" (*keiten aimin*); Itagaki, turning to new political rhetoric, called it "liberty," as in his famous utterance that Itagaki may die but liberty (*jiyū*) will not. Both men referred to the idealistic activism in restorationism and held strongly to the view that this spirit of loyal action was the fundamental nutritive ethic of the Japanese people, which ought to be nurtured where it was most consciously understood and maintained, namely among the former *samurai*. This point of view was compelling for many of the loyalists, and even Ōkubo, perhaps the staunchest "bureaucrat" of the new government, wavered in his pragmatic commitments. In 1874, he allowed the advocates of "action" a brief campaign against Formosa (in retaliation for the killing of Japanese fisher-

---

[4] On the debate among the loyalists leading up through the various rebellions, including Saigō's, see Masumi, *Nihon seitōshi ron*, vol. 1, pp. 115–212. The position of Itagaki and his friends from Tosa is documented in Itagaki Taisuke, *Jiyūtō shi*, 3 vols. (Tokyo: Iwanami shoten, 1958; first published in 1910). Good coverage of the politics of this entire period is found in Konishi Shirō, *Nihon zenshi*, vol. 8, *Kindai, 1* (Tokyo: Tokyo daigaku shuppankai, 1962), esp. pp. 319–53.

men), which in turn prompted Kido to resign, having bitterly accused Ōkubo of straying from his stated position.

In 1874–75, the loyalist leadership appeared momentarily splintered beyond recovery and incapable of maintaining itself as a viable governing elite. Of the prominent figures of the Restoration, only Ōkubo remained to hold the fragments of government together; and despite his stubborn strength and political acumen the situation seemed to point to certain political failure. It was in this context of grave pessimism and uncertainty that a decisive *rapprochement* was established in 1875 between Ōkubo and Kido in Osaka (*Osaka kaigi*). Through the mediating efforts of younger loyalists such as Itō Hirobumi and Inoue Kaoru (1835–1915), as well as Itagaki, the two leaders from Satsuma and Chōshū publicly reconfirmed their support of a constitutional system of government—*kokka rikken no seitai*. As a first step in this direction they agreed to the immediate establishment of prefectural assemblies and the drafting of a constitution.[5]

While a *rapprochement* between Ōkubo and Kido was possible since they shared much in common, and, similarly, an accommodation could be arranged between these two men and Itagaki and Gotō, who supported a party movement over violent rebellion, the split with Saigō, Maebara, and Etō was irreparable. Leading some 5,000 "patriots," Etō revolted in the "Saga Rebellion" of 1874. Ōkubo himself led the victorious government troops and ordered the execution of Etō. In Hagi, the castle town of Chōshū from which the final drive against the *bakufu* had been launched, Maebara raised his flag of revolt in 1876, only to be defeated and executed, an especially painful event for Chōshū loyalists in the government. And finally in 1877–78, Saigō led some 30,000 rebels in the "Satsuma Rebellion," fighting the new

[5] Andrew Fraser, "The Osaka Conference of 1875," *The Journal of Asian Studies* 16, no. 4 (August 1967): 589–610; and George Akita, *Foundations of Constitutional Government in Modern Japan, 1868–1900* (Cambridge: Harvard University Press, 1967), pp. 20–25. The latter is an important study of the politics of the 1870s and 1880s, skillfully written, especially concerning Itō Hirobumi. Also recommended is Nobutaka Ike, *The Beginnings of Political Democracy in Japan* (Baltimore: John Hopkins University Press, 1950).

conscript army for six months. Refusing surrender to his former comrades, Saigō, who with Ōkubo and Kido was one of the three major heroes of the Restoration, took his own life on the hill overlooking the castle town of Kagoshima.

For some five years, roughly between Saigō's departure from the government in 1873 and his defeat in 1878, some thirty rebellions were launched, mostly by former *samurai* who continued to exhibit an angry and resistant mood. In 1878, for example, a new artillery unit rioted in Tokyo, resulting in fifty-three executions (*Takehashi sōdō*). Ōkubo himself was assassinated in that same year by a rebellious former *samurai* from Ishikawa prefecture. Because this defiant activism was indeed close to a particular spiritual strand in restorationism, it was not the slain Ōkubo who emerged as the leading patriot of the Restoration, but men such as Etō, Maebara, and, especially, Saigō. Far from being remembered as a traitor, Saigō lived on as a crucial symbol of defiant loyalism in restorationism, in the tradition of Ōshio Heihachirō and Yoshida Shōin.

Clearly, however, with Saigō's defeat in the field of battle, "loyalism" could no longer mean "rebellion" in the sense that it had come to mean in the restorationist revolt against the *bakufu*. Political turmoil and violence persisted over the next ten years, but these were part of a movement of protest for popular rights and not organized military rebellions of the sort mounted by Saigō. The disputes now came to be focused primarily on the issues of designing the constitutional order, namely, the type of constitution and who should be responsible for drafting it.

The Establishment of Constitutional Government

Serious attention had been directed to the future structure of the "restored" political order even before the actual defeat of the *bakufu*. From the mid-1860s on into the 1870s, a dozen or so outlines were conceived. The better known of the earlier plans are Iwakura Tomomi's "Plan for National Unification" (*Zenkoku gōdōsaku*) and Sakamoto Ryōma's eight-point plan, sometimes called the "Tosa Plan" (*Tosa an*). Although these outlines are not especially impressive as legal documents, they indicate a growing awareness among loyalist leaders of the need for an authoritative reformulation of political structure. Sakamoto's, for example, lists two deliberative assemblies, government based on talent, reorganization of the military, and general fiscal reform that accords with the international gold standard.[6]

Nurtured in Tokugawa restorationist political thought, Meiji government leaders conceded that a well-formed bureaucratic structure was a fundamental precondition for the creation of wealth and power, and this view clearly underlay the appreciation for a Western "constitution" by men such as Kido, Ōkubo, Itō, Inoue, and others who accompanied the Iwakura Mission of 1871–1873 to observe and establish diplomatic relations with European nations and the United States.

Had Ōkubo and Kido lived into the 1880s, it is certain that their influence would have been decisive in drafting a constitution. Kido, however, died in 1877, and Ōkubo was assassinated just a year later. The actual task of shaping the new order went to younger loyalists: Itō Hirobumi, Yamagata Aritomo, and Inoue Kaoru from Chōshū; Matsukata Masayoshi (1835–1924) of Satsuma; and Ōkuma Shigenobu (1838–1922) from Hizen.[7] These men came into their own as loyalists when the rebellion against

[6] Jansen, *Sakamoto Ryōma*, pp. 335–40. See also Matsumoto, *Tennōsei kokka*, 118–253.

[7] Okuma Shigenobu, ed., *Fifty Years of New Japan*, 2 vols. (London: Smith, Elder, 1909). These volumes contain essays and reflections by leading figures of the Meiji era, including Itō and Yamagata. See also Akita, *Foundations of Constitutional Government*, especially for Itō; and Roger Hackett, *Yamagata Aritomo* (Cambridge: Harvard University Press, 1972). Henry Rosovsky and Kazushi Ohkawa touch on the significance of Matsukata Masayoshi in the area of economic development in "A Century of Japanese Economic Growth," in William W. Lockwood, ed., *The State and Economic Enterprise in Japan* (Princeton: Princeton University Press, 1965), pp. 47–92, esp. pp. 62–66. Good biographies are still lacking for Ōkuma Shigenobu and Inoue Kaoru. In Japanese, Oka Yoshitake has written a brilliant paperback, *Yamagata Aritomo* (Tokyo: Iwanami shoten, 1958); and he has written short pieces on Itō, Ōkuma, and others in *Kindai Nihon no seijika* (Tokyo: Bungeishunju, 1960).

the *bakufu* was virtually an accomplished fact. The search for an intellectual justification for revolt against the *bakufu* was not an issue with these men as earlier had been the case with Yoshida Shōin and Maki Izumi. They gained political maturity while planning the strategy of revolt and, more significantly, while translating that revolt into a lasting political achievement. In short, they were oriented toward organization. They agreed with Ōkubo and Kido that a constitutional government should replace the *bakufu* and clearly perceived the central role that the new bureaucratic system would play in Japan's development as a modern state.

Each of the young oligarchs left an indelible mark on the new political order. Yamagata, often characterized as the most "traditional" of the group, was instrumental in establishing the new system of military conscription, defeating Saigō in battle, and laying the foundation for "regional self-government" through which to mobilize and coordinate the resources of the country. Matsukata, drawing on the advice of Shibuzawa Eiichi, directed the economic breakthrough of the 1880s, especially through the establishment of a modern banking and investment structure anchored by the Bank of Japan. Inoue aided Itō in the drafting of the constitution and, in less-tangible yet equally important ways, mediated between government leaders and industrialists and contributed to the acceptance of these new economic figures as pillars of the modern order.

The most impressive figure of the group, however, was Itō Hirobumi. Following the demise of Kido and Ōkubo, and after a fierce struggle for power between himself and Ōkuma Shigenobu over the character of the new constitution, Itō established himself as the chief draftsman of the new constitution. Itō and Ōkuma had both served under Ōkubo and were equally committed to the idea of constitutional government. Both men were extremely able, intelligent, and ambitious politicians. Being from Chōshū, Itō had an advantage over Ōkuma, who came from Hizen, a lesser *han* in the restorationist movement. Due in part to this disadvantage, Ōkuma cultivated a power base of his own, drawing support from young university graduates (such as Yano Fumio [1850–1931], Ozaki Yukio [1859–1954], and Inukai Tsuyoshi [1855–1932]) and establishing ties with journalists, intellectuals, and industrialists in the emerging Mitsubishi combine. Ōkuma, however, erred in his tactic against Itō by the manner in which he proposed a constitution. Relying on a document drafted by men at Keio Academy (after 1920 Keio University) that drew heavily from the British constitutional system, Ōkuma, without first discussing the matter with Itō and others, petitioned the throne, urging the establishment of a constitutional order such as would be outlined by him within two years.

Itō retaliated swiftly. With the support of Iwakura, he rejected Ōkuma's proposal. The British constitution was "unwritten" and presumed to be distinctive to English political custom and, therefore, inconsistent with the Japanese national essence. The implications of this line of argument are readily evident: Having discarded much of medieval political history as "anachronistic" and "arbitrary," Japan was not in a sound position to rely on a constitution whose theoretical underpinning was customary law. What was required was an explicitly written constitution that would embody the authoritative norms of modern legal systems, and in this sense stand clearly in contrast to the history of *bakufu* governments since 1185; and, at the same time, allow within it the principle, as symbolized by the Japanese monarchy, of a distinctive and continuing cultural tradition.

The debate ended in clear victory for Itō. In 1881, under a glare of publicity, Ōkuma and his faction were compelled to resign from the government.[8] The debate, however, held new political significance for the 1880s and beyond. The contest between Ōkuma and Itō was between "bureaucrats," in contrast to the disputes in the 1870s between Kido and Ōkubo and Saigō,

---

[8] Akita, *Foundations*, pp. 31–66; and Andrew Fraser, "The Expulsion of Ōkuma from the Government in 1881," *The Journal of Asian Studies* 16, no. 2 (February 1967): 213–36. Akita focuses on the struggle between Itō and Ōkuma; Fraser emphasizes the changing character of politics on a broader plain. See also Masumi, *Nihon seitōshi*, vol. 2, pp. 5–20.

Maebara, Itagaki, and others over the fundamental meaning of the Restoration. Ōkuma did not agitate for rebellion from his regional home but remained in Tokyo where he founded Waseda, a leading private university to this day, and organized a "progressive" political party, the Kaishintō. Together with Itagaki's "Freedom Party," Jiyūtō, Ōkuma's Kaishintō contributed enormously toward an expanding arena of pragmatic politics outside of the oligarchy and included a complex social mixture of disgruntled former *samurai* (including previous servitors of the *bakufu*), taxpaying farmers, and city intellectuals, journalists, and industrialists. Although from different political bases, Itagaki having sided with Saigō and Ōkuma with Ōkubo, both men would lead an opposition party movement in the 1880s against the remaining oligarchs in power. Their activities as leaders of parties were new to modern Japan and would have been utterly unthinkable within the confines of the Tokugawa *bakufu*. In this respect, both Ōkuma and Itagaki were as important as the oligarchs in power in the creation of new institutions and organizations in modern Japanese politics.

It was Itō, however, possessing an unusual sense of political purpose and personal self-confidence, who was decisive in the final creation of the new constitutional order. Having met and overcome Ōkuma's challenge, Itō refused to be distracted from his personal task of drafting the new constitution. Returning home from a tour of Europe (1882–83) undertaken specifically to study Western constitutions, Itō was convinced of the appropriateness of the German constitutional model. The reasons for this choice are not difficult to discern, although Itō has been repeatedly criticized by historians for having erred in his choice. If the British model was not valid because of its identification with a distinctive history, the American system was less appropriate since it was a republic. Russia did not have a "constitution"; Italy's future as a constitutional monarchy seemed at best ambiguous; and France had had several constitutions and as many monarchs and pseudomonarchs since the French Revolution and had proven to be singularly ineffective in the Franco-Prussian War of 1870. By con-

trast, Germany was a newly unified nation. A constitution was
not part of its medieval political custom. Divided until recently
into principalities not unlike the *han* of Tokugawa times, it had
written a constitution explicitly to accord with the realization of
national unification. Within this constitutional framework, it had
industrialized in a relatively short time and had demonstrated its
strength against France in the field of battle. It was also indis-
putable that the theory of constitutionalism was being studied in
greater depth and sophistication in Germany than anywhere else
at the time.

Although confident of the German constitutional model, Itō
postponed the adoption of a constitution until the details of the
bureaucratic system had been worked out, a task he estimated
would take ten years and not two as Ōkuma proposed. Itō's tactic
was to "constitutionalize" a functioning bureaucracy as a *fait
accompli*. When the constitution was finally promulgated in
1889, a cabinet had been in operation for five years as the highest
executive body in the government; major ministries were locked
into place to handle taxes, defense, foreign relations, and domestic and regional affairs; the industrial revolution was well under-
way; a system of compulsory universal education and a national
university structure (capped by Tokyo Imperial University) was
operative and charged with the task of screening talent for the
new administrative and industrial bureaucracies. Itō's astuteness
lay in his perception of the role of a constitution in confirming
and legitimating an operative bureaucratic order; its function was
to "absolutize" political constructs after questions of power had
been settled and not to create new competitive power relations.

Working within the privy council, Itō drafted a constitution
based on a monarchical principle of hierarchy well known in
Tokugawa thought. Governmental hierarchy would terminate
with the monarchy, the *de jure* formative source of all legitimate
structures; at the same time, the monarchy would be the prime
focus of cultural identification, symbolizing a continuous history
and the nation's ideal of itself, a concept rendered in the pre-
amble with the familiar term *kokutai*, "national historical es-

sence." Because the monarchy was a constant referent point for both structure and culture, it would be "transcendent" of actual historical and political processes: It would remain "inactive," thus allowing loyal men throughout society to become maximally "active" in the world of practical and intellectual achievement. Although legal advisers such as Herman Roessler found this conception of monarchy highly inconsistent with Western constitutional theory (which indeed it was), Itō's view prevailed; thus the inclusion of stipulations in the constitution that the monarch shall rule within constitutional law, and that all ministers of state shall countersign and assume responsibility for cabinet-level decisions, which legally removed the monarchy from the realm of practical political action.

Below the monarchy and cabinet was a bicameral Diet. An upper house represented "blood," "wealth," and unusual "talent." This combination included peers (made up of former daimyō, Meiji leaders, and imperial relatives), who selected representatives from among themselves, men of wealth in the highest tax-paying brackets in the prefectures, who also selected their own representatives, and outstanding university scholars who were given special imperial appointments. A lower house represented "commoners," with suffrage extended to men paying a direct national tax of at least fifteen yen, a large amount that severely restricted the size of the electorate to barely one percent of the total population of 40 million. The lower house did not select the prime minister or members of the cabinet, a circumstance that curtailed its political power. But it possessed the right to initiate legislation and to approve the government's annual budget, both of which were important prerogatives. It also could exercise the right of interpellation, summoning cabinet ministers before the entire house to explain policy decisions and respond to direct questions. Finally, society in general was extended certain privileges within the legal order. There was a guarantee of equal protection under the law. A court system was established, which did not have the right of constitutional review (a function reserved for the privy council), but which was legally separate from the executive and legislative branches of the government. The principle of social mobility was confirmed, as were the prerogatives to buy, sell, move, choose one's occupation, publish, and worship in private.[9]

However important these personal privileges, especially for the formation of a highly pluralistic intellectual and cultural life for modern Japan, they should not be construed as the essential feature of the Meiji constitution. The document was not aimed at confirming a democratic ethic but was primarily an embodiment of the restorationist aspiration for a comprehensive and predictable legal system that would provide a final justification for the dissolution of the old order and the ushering in of a new and strong Japanese nation. Thus, violence against the new order was now rendered "unconstitutional," and "loyalism" as an unassailable virtue and ethic of action was "constitutionalized" to include the general citizenry. The privileges just mentioned, in short, were not aimed at supporting the ideal of human liberty and the right to protest, but the prerogative of all to participate in the creation of a strong society.

Guided by a pragmatic perception of politics, the oligarchs, and Itō especially, saw for modern Japan the need for absolute structures, bureaucratic edifices that would not change according to the whims of ambitious men between one generation and the next; but, in contrast to twentieth-century revolutionaries, they did not set out to provide a comprehensive intellectual "orthodoxy" with which to buttress the creation of a new constitutional order. Thus, aside from a few general and practical aims, the constitution did not provide a systematic political theory and ide-

[9] A translation of the Meiji Constitution (placed conveniently alongside the postwar constitution) is printed in Hugh Borton, *Japan's Modern Century* (New York: The Ronald Press Company, 1970; first published in 1955), pp. 569–88. See also Joseph Pittau, *Political Thought in Early Meiji Japan* (Cambridge: Harvard University Press, 1967), pp. 159–95. In Japanese: Nagai Hideo, "Meiji kempō seitei," *Iwanami kōza, Nihon rekishi*, vol. 16, *Kindai, 3* (Tokyo: Iwanami shoten, 1962), pp. 147–86; and Matsumoto, *Tennōseikokka*, pp. 254–94. The workings of the constitution are discussed in R. H. P. Mason, *Japan's First General Election, 1890* (London: Cambridge University Press, 1969); and in Bannō Junji, *Meiji kempō taisei no kakuritsu* (Tokyo: Tokyo daigaku shuppankai, 1971).

ology for modern Japan. For the most part, supportive ideology for constitutionalism came from sources outside the immediate circle of oligarchic leaders. The ideas offered were varied and the debates often fierce. In the end, a true political orthodoxy would not emerge from the discourse, although certain theories were more influential than others. All the ideas, however, supported the transformation of Japan from an agrarian and feudal order to a strong constitutional system. And although theoretically conflictive, these ideas would remain key themes in the development of a complex and critical tradition of constitutional thought and political criticism.

New Ideologies in the Meiji Era

Paralleling the effort to establish constitutional government was a wide variety of provocative intellectual attempts to provide new theories of action for the modern era. With the declassment and tumultuous change brought about by the Restoration, a good part of society, especially former *samurai* and the newly formed and heavily taxed landowners, appeared listless, disoriented, and angry. Many joined rebellions such as Saigō's or the protest movements of Itagaki and others, while a few struck out individually, as in the assassination of Ōkubo. A rowdy mood persisted below the immediate surface of rational institutional building in economic and political fields well into the 1880s. Much political thought in the Meiji era addressed itself to this apparent discrepancy between radical and unexpected disruption in history (which necessarily redefined the content and quality of action) and the continuing psychological attachment to loyal action as a social value.

It is precisely in the context of this perceived discrepancy that the unusually intense engagement with Western ideas at this time should be understood. It was not simple cultural mimesis or pure intellectual curiosity that led to the incorporation of Western ideas, but a strongly felt need for intellectual order in a context of grave psychological uncertainty. Western ideas provided a contrast to the prevailing ideology of the immediate past that had been severely undermined by the restoration movement and for which distrust had deepened; and they could provide, therefore, new focus and meaning to a widely shared determination to contribute to the nation's survival in a dangerously competitive world.

Three modes of political thought are especially significant to the Meiji era: first, the materialistic liberalism of Fukuzawa Yukichi (1834–1901) and Nishi Amane (1829–97); second, natural-right thought, as expressed by Ueki Emori (1857–92) and Nakae Chōmin (1847–1901); and third, the idealistic theory of social evolution identified with Katō Hiroyuki (1836–1916) and Nishimura Shigeki (1828–1902). Although these ideologies shared certain intellectual views each had a qualitatively different impact on modern Japan. For example, Fukuzawa's ideas meshed with and provided permissive reinforcement for the cult of success, mobility, and entrepreneurial hustle that permeated all levels of Meiji society; those of Ueki and Nakae reaffirmed the need for idealistic protest for modern Japan; and Katō's provided a new synthesis between history and the present, redefining the importance of loyalism despite the great changes of the recent past.

Ueki and Nakae were from Itagaki's home, Tosa, and came to be identified as the intellectual leadership of Itagaki's party, the Jiyūtō, and, more generally, of the popular-rights movement, that had risen in protest against the new oligarchs in power. The others, Fukuzawa, Nishi, Katō, and Nishimura, gained fame as leading members of a society of intellectual publicists called the Meiji Six Society (*Meirokusha*). It was this society, formed six years after the Restoration, that initiated through discussion and publication a crucial movement to bring "cultural clarification" and "enlightenment" (*bummei; keimō*) to modern Japan.

The men of this society were the very best of a stratum of restless and individualistic *samurai*-intellectuals in late Tokugawa. Even as they gave loyal service as bureaucrats, they had gained a certain objectivity toward feudal structures and commitments that bore a striking resemblance to the earlier politically active loyalists, and they were quickly accepted by the new leaders in the Meiji government as colleagues and special advisers. These men came from different parts of the country—Fukuzawa from the modern-day Ōita prefecture in western Japan and Katō from near the city of Kōbe, for example—but they generated a common esprit among themselves as specialists in Western literature, being especially proficient in Dutch, English, and German. Due to their special skills they attracted the attention of the great late Tokugawa scholar Sakuma Shōzan, a servitor of the *bakufu*, who employed them in a bureau of the *bakufu* that handled Western books. Some accompanied *bakufu* envoys to Europe and America as translators or to stay on as students of Western legal systems. By 1868 they were already mature intellectuals, scholars, and, above all, publicists. Katō's work of 1862, "The Grasses Next Door" (*Tonarigusa*), while ostensibly discussing the lack of constitutional regularity in Chinese politics, was actually a denunciation of the *bakufu* he served. Fukuzawa's "Conditions in the West" (*Seiyō jijō*) of 1866 and "An Encouragement of Learning" (*Gakumon no susume*) of 1872 both pointed to the dawning of a new Japan over the feudal past and were enormously popular classics all through the Meiji era, their total sales soaring into several million copies.

Immediately following the Restoration, the members of the Meiji Six Society stood on common ground in their iconoclasm toward history and agreement on the need for cultural disengagement with the immediate past.[10] Indulging in what seems in retrospect oversimplification, they singled out the metaphysical ethics of Neo-Confucianism as the governing absolute in the tra-

10 All of the issues of the journal *Meiroku zasshi* have been reproduced in vol. 18 of Yoshino Sakuzō, ed., *Meiji bunka zenshū*, 24 vols. (Tokyo: Meiji bunka kenkyūkai, 1927–29). A good discussion is Matsumoto Sannosuke, *Kindai Nihon no seiji to ningen* (Tokyo: Sōbunsha, 1966), pp. 3–60; and also Ōkubo Toshiaki, "Meirokusha no hitobito," in Konishi, ed., *Nihon jimbutsushi taikei*, vol. 5, pp. 123–54. A useful volume in English is Masaaki Kosaka, *Japanese Thought in the Meiji Era*, translated and adapted by David Abosch (Tokyo: Pan-Pacific Press, 1958).

ditional order and, relying on arguments not entirely unknown in Tokugawa thought, leveled their polemical attack against that structure of thought. They noted that a crucial distinction was not made in Neo-Confucian metaphysical ethics between the principles of nature and of social ethics, so that natural principles were made to appear moral and secular ethics and institutions were erroneously rendered sacrosanct according to unchanging norms in nature. Due to this intellectual confusion, the development of Japan was severely arrested, especially in contrast to the West, where, during the Enlightenment of the eighteenth century, men were liberated from social constructs and a religious view of nature and given an autonomous significance and power to create a new future. Superstitious dogma was replaced by a quest for scientific principles that might be applied to social development. Rejecting truths as historically given, the Enlightenment offered the possibility of a progressive future.

The intellectual use of the Enlightenment as an antithetical universal to Neo-Confucian metaphysical ethics was extremely convenient and effective. The past, as a total ideological reality, could be discredited by an alternative set of assumptions that appeared to mesh with the realities of postrestoration Japan. Beyond an initial polemical usefulness, however, the concept of the Enlightenment as an alternative ideology underwent swift erosion. The Enlightenment, after all, was not an internally coherent conceptual construct, but highly pluralistic and indicative of more than a single set of ideas. Similarly, beginning in the mid-1870s, there developed sharply divergent views regarding what should be the proper ideological foundation of modern Japan. Fukuzawa insisted on a pragmatic and empiricist point of view; advocates of natural right, Ueki and Nakae, intervened with intriguing idealistic concepts about individual spiritual autonomy as the basis of popular government; while Katō supported with unusual strength of mind a view of the nation-state based on the theory of social evolution and national survival.

In a manner without precedent, Fukuzawa reduced society to

autonomous individuals.[11] His reasons were uncomplicated: Provided that men do not accept a priori ethical absolutes, they can continue to create history; history, without such absolutes, is a continuing accumulation of relative creations that form the basis for self-reliant cultures. As in much of British utilitarian thought, into which he read deeply, Fukuzawa accepted as a *sine qua non* the ultimate convergence of individual activity into a larger national society. Due to an excessive historical identification with Chinese culture, he reasoned, the Japanese had been constrained from creating a strong and autonomous nation. Yet perhaps most crucial in Fukuzawa was the curious combination of hedonism and idealism in his understanding of the new individualism for modern Japan.

Individual autonomy, he contended, rests on the rational pursuit of self-interest. As in British philosophic radicalism, Fukuzawa pointed to self-awareness of personal well-being, including the possession of material comforts, as the minimum criterion for judging the validity of action. He accepted this radical materialism as the key theoretical antithesis to Neo-Confucian metaphysical absolutism and as the building block of subsequent social creation. Yet, the psychic energy with which men seek the creative

[11] Some of Fukuzawa's writings have been translated into English: *The Autobiography of Fukuzawa Yukichi*, trans. Eiichi Kiyooka (Tokyo: Hokuseido Press, 1960; first published in 1934); *An Encouragement of Learning*, trans. David A. Dilworth and Umeyo Hirano (Tokyo: Sophia University Press, 1969); and *An Outline of a Theory of Civilization*, trans. David A. Dilworth and G. Cameron Hurst (Tokyo: Sophia University Press, 1973). Also of interest are Carmen Blacker, *The Japanese Enlightenment* (London: Cambridge University Press, 1964); Albert M. Craig, "Fukuzawa Yukichi: The Philosophical Foundations of Meiji Nationalism," in Robert E. Ward, ed., *Political Development in Modern Japan* (Princeton: Princeton University Press 1969), pp. 99–148; and Irwin Scheiner, *Christian Converts and Social Protest in Meiji Japan* (Berkeley: University of California Press, 1970), pp. 193–224 passim. Two stimulating essays in Japanese are Maruyama Masao "Fukuzawa Yukichi no tetsugaku," in Hidaka Rokurō, ed., *Gendai Nihon shisōtaikei*, vol. 34, *Kindaishugi* (Tokyo: Chikuma Shobō, 1964), pp. 58–92; and Ienaga Saburō, *Kindai Nihon no shisōka* (Tokyo: Yūshindō, 1962), pp. 71–84.

satisfaction of the self was an internal spiritual power and potential, which Bentham, or for that matter Ogyū, from whom much materialistic thought in Japan is derived, would have defined as the instinct for passionate aggrandizement. For Fukuzawa, this spiritual potential must be liberated because of its constructive power. For him "happiness" lay not so much in the actual possession of a pleasurable object, but in the uncompromising and dedicated commitment to pursue whatever goal the individual has defined for himself as worthy of acquiring. He referred to this spirit as the power of self-endurance (*yasegaman*), the commitment to struggle as an individual even against insurmountable odds.

It was obviously the spirit of the *samurai*-intellectual which was now being made to mesh with a legitimate hedonism in the calculated pursuit of self-interest. It was not contradictory for Fukuzawa to admire Saigō Takamori, the rebellious idealist of the Meiji Restoration, while strongly advocating modern parliamentary government to regulate the spirited expression of self-interest. In Fukuzawa, the principles of "utility" and "action" that we have seen woven into the political culture of late Tokugawa and early Meiji were combined to encourage individuals throughout Meiji society to educate themselves, rise up in the world, and gain national fame (rendered *risshin shusse*, the slogan of Fukuzawa's day). An enormously successful pundit, critic, and educator, Fukuzawa played a pivotal role in the formulation and diffusion of an entrepreneurial ethic for modern Japan that has clearly withstood the test of time.

A special point needs to be made about the relationship between early Meiji materialism and British utilitarianism. Materialism was not discovered in the West, it being deeply rooted in much of rationalistic Tokugawa thought, as in the tradition of Ogyū. It was British utilitarianism, and Continental positivism, however, that redirected Tokugawa materialism from a theory of political hierarchy to an intellectual confirmation of the individualized pursuit of self-interest.

This process is observable in Nishi Amane,[12] a colleague of Fukuzawa. Nishi's break with Neo-Confucian metaphysics was made in the early 1850s after a close reading of Ogyū's writings. The distinction Ogyū made between nature and ethics as generically distinguishable spheres of reality made a deep impact on Nishi, so that even after his tour of Europe in the early 1860s and after the Restoration, he still continued to work with Ogyū's rational thought. Even his imagery of government as being structured with beams consciously fashioned by men for social ends was almost certainly drawn from Ogyū's "discrimination of the way" (Bendō). Yet, as with Fukuzawa, it was Western utilitarian and empirical thought that turned Nishi's understanding of Ogyū's rational materialism into a theory of general social progress. While Ogyū saw only the sage-king or extraordinary genius as endowed with creative perception, Nishi and Fukuzawa generalized this potential to include the lower classes in society. Thus, while Ogyū stressed structured social order (ammin), Nishi recast this as social "happiness." On the basis of rational psychological perception, Nishi reasoned, men can choose and decide what is beneficial for themselves, and therefore, men need not be merely passive recipients of external norms (yorashimubeshi, as Ogyū had taught) but active elements in the creation of a better society.

Rejecting metaphysical schemes of thought and deemphasizing historical ideology, then, both Fukuzawa and Nishi endorsed the empirical, or sensate, basis of knowledge. Claiming that this empiricism allowed men to make rational choices in the present, including the pursuit of concrete self-interest, Fukuzawa and Nishi predicted future national strength and social well-being. Yet, both men were vulnerable for the same reason: How would men truly know what autonomous "self-interest" was if knowledge is post-experience, shaped by an external and preexisting social environment?

[12] Thomas R. H. Havens, Nishi Amane and Modern Japanese Thought (Princeton: Princeton University Press, 1970). A useful general coverage is Hashikawa Bunzō and Matsumoto Sannosuke, eds., Kindai Nihon seiji shisōshi, 2 vols. (Tokyo: Yūhikaku, 1971), vol. 1, pp. 151–158 and 166–78.

Fukuzawa tended to think the capacity for independent judgment was an irreducible "right" (*kenri*), as proposed by the natural-right theory. In one of the popular phrases of the day coined by him, Fukuzawa observed that Heaven or Nature did not create men above or below others, suggesting a natural basis of human equality and individuality. In this respect, he seems squarely in the camp of natural-right theorists and, indeed, there was a good deal in common in their political views. On closer observation, however, Fukuzawa was not an unequivocal proponent of natural rights. He consistently stressed the hedonistic propensity of men as the basis of individual choice, and his idea of "liberty" was actually a psychological power to "endure" that is conceptually distinguishable from the theory of natural rights. In Nishi, too, judgmental autonomy was defined in terms of psychological perception (*shinri*), rather than an innate right existing prior to experience.

Distinguisable from Fukuzawa's and Nishi's hedonism and utilitarianism were proponents of a natural-right theory, such as Ueki Emori and Nakae Chōmin.[13] Both Ueki and Nakae gained fame as intellectual leaders of the popular-rights movement which reached its climax in the years 1881–85 in the form of radical protest demonstrations against the oligarchs in Osaka, Tokyo, Fukushima, Chichibu, and various other parts of the country. Ueki and Nakae sought the establishment of a popularly elected system of parliamentary government (*minsen giin*) based on the theory of

---

[13] Pittau, *Political Thought*, pp. 99–130. The principal intellectuals of the popular-rights movement are discussed by Tōyama Shigeki, "Minken undō no hitobito." Konishi, ed., *Nihon jimbutsushi taikei*, vol. 5, pp. 155–84; Gotō Yasuji, "Jiyū to minken no shisō," *Iwanami kōza, Nihon rekishi*, vol. 16, *Kindai*, 3 (Tokyo: Iwanami shoten, 1962), pp. 147–86. Hashikawa and Matsumoto, eds., *Kindai Nihon seiji shisōshi*, vol. 1, pp. 180–205. Ienaga Saburō discusses Ueki in *Kindai Nihon no shisōka*, pp. 85–98; and Hayashi Shigeru discusses Nakae Chōmin in *Kindai Nihon no shisōka tachi* (Tokyo: Iwanami shoten, 1958), pp. 10–69. Ueki's key works, *Minken jiyū ron* and *Tempu jinken ben*, are anthologized in *Meiji bunka zenshū*, vol. 5; and Nakae's *Sansuijin keirin mondō* is in ibid, vol. 7. For other important intellectuals in the popular-rights movement, see Marius B. Jansen, "Ōi Kentarō: Radicalism and Chauvinism," *Far Eastern Quarterly* no. 11, 3 (May 1952): 305–16; and also Hagihara Nobutoshi, *Baba Tatsui* (Tokyo: Chuōkoronsha, 1970).

natural right and popular sovereignty but failed to get their ideas incorporated into the Meiji constitution. Although historians are often quick to point out their political failure, their importance lies in the intellectual effort they spearheaded in conceptually redefining the indigenous tradition of idealistic action.

Both Ueki and Nakae sought to establish a credible intellectual link between dedicated individual action and "true principle" (*seiri*) and to redefine this relationship as a natural possession or "right" of all men. In this respect, their effort parallels that of Fukuzawa to generalize theoretical materialism from its elitist and authoritarian uses in the past to a mode of popular thought and action. Ueki, for example, argued that the flaw in traditional idealism was its moral elitism: Action was conceptualized as a sagely activity to "save" the people from their misery, as in the archetypical case of Ōshio Heihachirō. Noble action consisted of the enlightened few responding to external evils in history. A viable theory of action, however, should be valid without regard to empirical perceptions of specific conditions. The theory of natural right was decisive as a mediating concept, for it could be applied to generalize an elitist view of action into a "popular" imperative for political participation. Everyone ought to act not because of turmoil, misery, and uncertainty in the present, but because internal convictions are consistent with a higher normative principle of nature.

While directed to society in general, the above message was most keenly received by declassed former *samurai*. Despite their loss of status and wealth, they could identify with a persuasive thought that said they ought not act out of despair with their lot but with spiritual conviction that was in accordance with a natural principle of action (*hōri* and *tenrikōdō* are often-used terms). Moreover, because the right to action was defined as natural to everyone, declassment must be accepted as irreversible, and an identification with feudal aristocracy, as expressed in military rebellion by and for the elite (such as in Saigō's uprising), must be eliminated from the modern political scene. Through the theory of natural right, then, the bruising psychological reality of declassment was explained as part of progress, the poverty of military rebellion was exposed, and the value of loyal action was directed toward participation in a radical popular movement.

Central to this Meiji natural-right thought was the concept of perfect individual autonomy, which was understood to be "natural" and the basis of self-power and self-reliance, or *jiriki*, a deeply religious idea in Japanese tradition. Unrelated to structures of power, this spiritual autonomy was also free of *passion*. It was, despite Ueki's claims to the contrary, a moral principle, "liberté morale" in the words of Nakae Chōmin, but expressed and understood as a "still" and "imperturbable" spiritual power (not unlike Fukuzawa's ideal of "endurance") that is closely related to ideas in Mencius and in Zen and Ōyōmei. As already observed in the case of Ueki, however, the elitism of this complex tradition was rejected as inadequate for modern Japan. The concept of "contract" played a crucial role here.

Drawing obviously from Rousseau, Nakae and others emphasized that, being naturally autonomous and free, men have the capacity to regulate themselves and the relationships among themselves through contract. Although a certain amount of personal freedom is curbed, this is necessary for the well-being of society as a whole. Above all, they stressed the "heaven-given right" (*tempujinken*) of everyone to participate in a system of popular representation. The aims of this participation were twofold: first, to provide for self-regulation, the people deciding, by and for themselves as to what was good and proper; second, to guard constantly against unprincipled and despotic leadership. Men lose their natural freedom to bureaucratic despotism, as the history of Japan showed. But in revolution, the natural freedom of men could be "restored" through the formulation of a new legal "contract." It followed that the Meiji Restoration (including the subsequent destruction of feudal constructs) was such a revolutionary turning point. It also followed that the bureaucratic oligarchs in power had betrayed the principle of the Restoration by not establishing popular government and therefore ought to be criticized and resisted through an articulate political movement.

In this manner, the disruptions of recent history were explained, as was the need for continuing and uncompromising action within a movement of protest. Clearly, natural-right theory played an extremely crucial role in providing new explanatory sophistication and a broader social significance to a widely understood and indigenously grounded concept of idealistic moral action. It helped to shift the focus of discontented former *samurai* from rebellion to a movement of protest for parliamentary government; and in so doing provided existing conceptions of radical protest with a language and theory utterly pertinent and relevant to the present and distinct and disengaged from the opprobrious connotations of "feudal" behavior.

Whether lecturing at rallies on the rectitude of equal treatment for women and outcastes, as by Ueki and Nakae, or debating the position that popular sovereignty led inevitably to national power (*minken-kokken*), as by Itagaki and Ōi Kentarō (1843–1922), the advocates of natural rights consistently sought to give new and optimistic theoretical meaning to the tradition of loyal activism. Their ideology was perhaps best documented in Nakae's justly famous "Discourse among Three Drunkards" (*Sansuijin keirinmondō*, 1887). Here he allowed himself to argue, as one of the "drunkards," the possibility of the steady expansion of human freedom in modern Japan through intellectual dispute and political struggle, even though objective conditions, including the constitutional order, might turn out to be far less than ideal. The importance of natural-right thought in Meiji Japan, then, was that it provided optimistic intellectual meaning, and hence also psychological sustenance, for an action-oriented and literate political stratum caught in extraordinary historical fluctuations.

Against both utilitarian and natural-right thought, a sharply contrasting position was formulated by Katō Hiroyuki and Nishimura Shigeki. They discredited the concept of rational self-interest as untenable and having little sustained value for society, and they rejected as faulty the reasoning that the allowance of popular rights leads inevitably to national strength. In 1882, Katō presented his basic views in an enormously important work entitled

"A New Thesis on Human Rights" (*Jinken shinsetsu*).[14] Arguing that human personality was not natural but shaped by the social environment, and hence by historical culture, Katō sought to give new significance to the concept of a distinctive Japanese cultural tradition to conform with the needs of the postrestoration era. Not seeking a simple revival of historical myths, Katō employed the concept of national historical essence (*kokutai*), to emphasize how the present might be comprehended (and hence controlled) in the light of continuing change and development. In particular, Katō injected a new idealistic principle of achievement into the concept of Japan's historical essence to confirm the continuing validity of loyal action on behalf of society. The unprecedented rebellion of 1868 is thus seen as such an achievement and, despite its absence in the past, the idea of a modern constitution as a "contract" (*ritsuyaku*) is also endorsed as valid in the evolutiontary process of the Japanese nation. It is this evolution of social history, Katō argued, that continuously defines and redefines the character of loyal action in time, giving social purpose to action despite specific changes in the activities themselves. Whereas self-interest could not define social purpose, his concept of evolution could be made to show how a moment of action is connected with a progressive sequence, and thus takes on predictive significance.

A crucial point for Katō was that while historical change was inevitable, social survival was neither natural nor necessary. Survival required conscious commitment and effort on behalf of a social principle that transcended the immediate needs of the present, and was indeed embedded in history itself. For while all societies may be thought of as evolving social entities, they developed qualitatively distinctive historical personalities. In arguing in

[14] Pittau, *Political Thought*, pp. 55–65 and passim; and Sansom, *The Western World and Japan*, pp. 434–37. See also Matsumoto, *Kindai Nihon no seiji to ningen*, pp. 61–92. Katō's *Tonarikusa* is in Matsumoto Sannosuke, ed., *Gendai Nihon shisō taikei*, vol. 1, *Kindai shisō no hōga* (Tokyo: Chikuma shobō, 1966), pp. 278–95; and his *Jinken shinsetsu* is in *Nihon bunka zenshū*, vol. 5.

this manner, Katō reopened the gates of history: The uncomfortable question now needed to be asked, despite the memory of the recent rejection of feudal ideology, how might the past be linked to the future? Historical ethics must be re-examined and viable and dynamic concepts extracted to create a nutritive ethic for the modern world and link the present to a continuing history.

The implications of Katō's view can be seen in the synthesis formulated by Nishimura Shigeki,[15] an original member of the Meiji Six Society who shared many of Katō's ideas. In two treatises of great importance, both published in 1886, "On Japanese Morality" and "On the Moral Reconstruction of the Nation," (*Nihon dōtokuron; Dōtoku rikkokuron*), Nishimura spelled out his ideas about the moral foundation of Japan as a modern nation. He called for a new ethic that combined Confucian humanism and Western scientific positivism. The strength of positivism, he reasoned, was its scientific management of social progress. The empirical and logical methods of positivism were indispensable to modern life, although it failed to explain adequately the moral character of human intention and therefore was not convincing in defining the proper ends that society ought to achieve. Confucianism, on the other hand, was seriously flawed. Its emphasis on blood, kinship, genealogy, on superiors over inferiors and men over women, the exaggerated glorification of the ancient world, and, above all, an erroneous sense of cultural superiority, were all untenable for modern Japan. Moreover, it lacked a scientific method and the idea of progress. Yet Confucianism communicated an essential ethical truth that ought not be discarded: It taught that the meaning of social life lay not in seeking salvation in another world (as taught in Christianity and Buddhism) but in cultivating relationships among members of society built on trust, a fundamental sense of one's humaneness, and, above all, a

15 On Nishimura Shigeki, see Donald H. Shively, "Nishimura Shigeki: A Confucian View of Modernization," in Marius B. Jansen, ed., *Changing Japanese Attitudes toward Modernization* (Princeton: Princeton University Press, 1965), pp. 193–241. Nishimura's *Nihon dōtokuron* appeared in paperback form in 1935 (Tokyo: Iwanami shoten) and was republished in 1963. Nishimura's writings are collected in Nihon kōdōkai, ed., *Hakuō sōshō*, 2 vols. (Tokyo: Nihon kōdōkai, 1912).

commitment to loyal action on behalf of others. It was this secular ethic, Nishimura concluded, that should be reintegrated as a nutritive value into modern Japanese life.

Like Katō, Nishimura was obviously not a blind traditionalist seeking the restoration of an idyllic past. His eyes were clearly focused on the psychological present in which he perceived with renewed significance and force the importance of a spiritual ethic in the new world of industrialization and constitutional bureaucracy. Yet, shorn of theoretical premises and sophisticated reasoning, his conclusions would be reworked, indeed in good part through his own efforts as adviser to the oligarchs, into the Imperial Rescript on Education of 1890 and disseminated through the new system of universal compulsory education as guidelines for loyal and patriotic action on behalf of the national good.

Through Katō and Nishimura, the quest for ideological certitude made a complete swing from intellectual iconoclasm to modern conservatism. Through them the importance of history was affirmed as a decisive principle for social survival and development. And their views did provide new focus and direction for loyalism, being far less vulnerable intellectually than rational hedonism, which could be made to appear a luxury for a society still uncertain about its own survival.

Despite the officially favored position of Katō and Nishimura against the theories of rational self-interest and natural right, the latter two ideas remained important as intellectual themes in modern Japan. The ethic of personal advancement that Fukuzawa encouraged remained a deeply ingrained legacy of the Meiji era, presenting a contrastive face to the more austere ethic developed by Katō, or, for that matter, Ueki and Nakae. The spirit of radical protest fostered by Ueki and Nakae in the popular-rights movement likewise survived, although it underwent significant reformulation in the twentieth century under nationalist and socialist points of views. Movements of protest in the twentieth century identified explicitly with men such as Ueki and Nakae in arguing for democratic and social reform. The point should be underscored, however, that all three systems of thought treated here shared certain common underlying aims that, despite contrasting theoretical assumptions, tended to be supportive of Japan's drastic transformation following the Restoration of 1868.

All three endorsed industrialism and constitutional government over feudal agrarianism and *bakufu* despotism. All three viewed the Restoration as a fundamental break with the past. Yet, in qualitatively different ways, each made selective use of history to help further the development of Japan. Katō's use of national essence, Fukuzawa's reference to the psychology of endurance, and Ueki's discussion of the tradition of moral protest, all bear out this general point. Most important, all three attempted to arrive at a new intellectual integration for the modern era, a point that should not be obscured by their widely varied theoretical constructs. Each sought to provide cogent explanation for and intelligibility to a chaotic present. From different perspectives, they sought to give broad social significance to an existing ethic of action (*jissen rinri*), including its idealism, its spirit of commitment, and its competitive energy, and to provide intellectual purpose and direction within a new "contractual" or constitutional order.

In their search for an intellectual structure for the present, Fukuzawa, Nakae, and Katō parallelled Itō, Yamagata, Matsukata, and the other oligarchs in the construction of a stable political order. Their concern was not with strategies of revolt, as had been the case with the preceding generation, but with shaping the present and defining the future, the underlying issue of much of the political disputes of the period. Intellectual leaders and oligarchs alike shared a common spirit: Whether in the construction of a university by Fukuzawa (Keiō), the formation of political parties by Ōkuma and Itagaki, the establishment of modern industries by Iwasaki of Mitsubishi, choosing the career of publicist as in the case of Katō and Ueki, or the drafting of a constitution by Itō, all seem to exhibit a common ambitious, entrepreneurial spirit that was distinctive to the culture of their day. It was a spirit that went beyond the confines of commerce and included political and intellectual activity, and may indeed be thought of as the sustaining ethos in the Meiji search for national certitude.

By the end of the nineteenth century, the revolutionary era of the Meiji Restoration had clearly come to an end. Itō saw good reason to look back with some pride over the thirty years following the Restoration and observe that men could now properly concentrate on making the constitutional system work for the good of the nation. All the oligarchs shared this "authoritarian" view of the constitution. Constitutional politics for them did not mean legal sanction for contention between rival interest and ideological groupings, but, quite the contrary, it was expected to reduce strife and create consensus. The constitution, of course, did not function as harmoniously as Itō expected. The parties behaved rambunctiously in the Diet. And although Katō, Fukuzawa, and Nakae endorsed the constitution, they did so for different reasons, as the previous discussion suggested. For Katō, the constitutional order define devoted action for society; for Fukuzawa, it legitimated disputes based on self-interest and allowed for orderly change; for Nakae, it legalized the struggle to expand freedom in society. Whatever feeling of certainty that Itō and his colleagues might have had was short-lived indeed. As political struggle and intellectual debate persisted unabated, Itō himself was forced to change his views on how the constitutional system should work, involving himself in a deep and bitter dispute with Yamagata, and finally, in 1900, becoming president of a political party in the Diet.

In short, the Meiji legacy to the twentieth century was not one of harmony but of great contention. In 1900, the intellectual fabric of society was decidedly pluralistic, lacking a commanding ideological orthodoxy. In the next several decades up to the eve of the Pacific War the intellectual divisions deepened and took on forms of strenuous criticism and protest against the quality of political life, while the constitutional system itself underwent dramatic change from within, especially in regard to constitutional thought and power relationships, and moved in a direction quite unintended by the men who fashioned the Meiji constitutional settlement.

5

Political Change and Protest
in the Early Twentieth Century

The thought and movement behind the Meiji Restoration in the Tokugawa period began the modernization of Japan, but the momentum was abruptly broken with an abortive second movement, the so-called "Shōwa Restoration" of the 1930s, in the decade preceding the Pacific War. While the Meiji Restoration led to the dissolution of the feudal order and unleashed competitive energies throughout the country in the diverse fields of education, industry, and politics, restorationism in the twentieth century did not result in institutional breakthroughs but in outrageous behavior by extreme nationalists and military men at home and abroad, causing unprecedented social misery. Although armed with elaborate and detailed plans for "national reconstruction" (*kokka kaizō*) to rectify bureaucratic ineffectualness, corruption, and injustice, the second restoration did not physically alter the existing constitutional structures. What it did do was challenge that order from within and cripple it, throwing bureaucratic leadership into disarray and confusing its identification with constitutional ideology. Thus, while a sense of the splendor and adventure of the Meiji Restoration remains etched in the social imagination of the

Japanese, the second restoration is universally denounced as an Asian variant of international fascism and as modernization that somehow went wrong.

The history that links the constitutional settlement of 1889 and the turmoil of the 1930s is not an easy story to relate. Society was severely strained as the population doubled, the industrial revolution advanced, unabated, and industry decisively outstripped agriculture (leading to a steady decline of the regions in demographic and cultural power as against the cities), mass culture and modern forms of hedonism spread with conspicuous vigor through much of urban society, and parliamentary politics appeared to intellectual leaders in the country to be hopelessly mired in corruption. Above all, there was growing disagreement on the nation's future direction. Although discourse on the subject began well back in the Meiji era, it was especially after Japan's military victory over Russia in 1905 that the discussions turned into conflicting criticisms of the constitutional settlement and debates over what constitutionalism should achieve for society. There followed intense introspection about the proper historical impact of the Meiji Restoration on the country's headlong plunge into industrialism. This introspection used a variety of conceptual languages that continued the highly diverse intellectual tradition of Meiji: popular nationalism (*minzokushugi*); democratic liberalism (*mimponshugi*); socialism (*shakaishugi*); and, as suggested, defiant restorationism.

Furthermore, what makes this history especially difficult to explain is that the constitutional order did not remain static as an unchanging target of attack. Indeed, beginning in the early twentieth century, the political and ideological character of the constitutional order underwent substantial redefinition. Through party politics in the hands of Hara Kei (1866–1921) and the political theory of Minobe Tatsukichi (1873–1948), the constitution was given new significance and pointed in a direction that Itō Hirobumi and his coterie of friends in the 1890s had not envisioned. By triggering a variety of responses regarding the proper nature of constitutional government, both Hara and Minobe are significant to the twentieth-century history of disagreement, contention, and declining political certainty.

CONSTITUTIONAL POLITICS AND IDEOLOGY

Despite a universal acceptance of the Meiji constitution when it was first promulgated, politics within that framework were far from harmonious. All through the 1890s, and on into the early decades of the twentieth century, fierce political competition and struggle developed that extensively changed the character of Japanese constitutional politics.

Within the oligarchy, for example, a tension between Itō and Yamagata Aritomo flared into the open in the early 1890s that intensified in the course of the decade.[1] Although both men had served under Ōkubo Toshimichi and shared a bureaucratic view of Japanese politics, they had a fundamental disagreement on the role of the new constitution. Primarily a military figure, Yamagata saw the constitution as a framework for social mobilization akin to the system of military conscription he had designed. Party opposition and protest differed little from rebellious disturbances, which, in his eyes, the constitution had now defined to be treasonous. By contrast, Itō opposed the use of military and police force to regulate domestic politics. An astute observer of historical trends, Itō was convinced that the use of force was counterproductive to the achievement of those national goals he and Yamagata were agreed upon. Not a liberal in an ideological sense, Itō nonetheless believed in making the constitution "functional" and adaptive and not suppressive of opposition groups and movements. Thus, in 1892, Itō objected to Yamagata's endorsement of police interference at the polls; several years later he maneuvered to have his former rival Ōkuma Shigenobu, head of

[1] See Oka Yoshitake on Itō in *Kindai Nihon no seijika*, pp. 9–47; and Tokinoya Masaru and Umetani Noboru, "Itō Hirobumi to Yamagata Aritomo," in Ōkubo Toshiaki, ed., *Nihon jimbutsushi taikei*, vol. 6, *Kindai*, 2 (Tokyo: Asakura shoten 1960), pp. 231–57; and Masumi, *Nihon seitōshi ron*, vol. 2, pp. 292–393.

one of the major parties, the Kaishintō, appointed as prime minister; and in 1900 he himself assumed the presidency of the Seiyūkai, the other principal party in the lower house. While Itō adapted in this manner, exhibiting a growing realization of the great importance of the parties in the constitutional order, Yamagata remained adamantly opposed to them. As a strenuous objection to Itō's tactics, Yamagata forged a formidable alliance of conservatives in the upper reaches of the bureaucracy, the privy council, the house of peers, and in the prefectural governments. This group of men, known as the "Yamagata faction," came to dominate the political system in the early 1900s, frustrating Itō and driving him away from the center of politics in Tokyo to take on the governor-generalship of Korea, where he was assassinated by a Korean nationalist in 1909.

A more visible political competition was that which arose within the party movement.[2] Here, too, the contention centered on the meaning of constitutional politics. One segment, led by Inukai Tsuyoshi, Ozaki Yukio and others, urged the establishment and maintenance of a union of popular parties (*daidōdanketsu*), initially envisioned in the popular-rights movement of the 1880s, which would compel the oligarchs, and the Yamagata faction especially, to accede to party cabinets responsible to the lower house. Specifically, a unified lower house could reject the government's budget and harass the cabinet with its right of interpellation. This general tactic naturally depended on an idealistic esprit. Of the three demands by the parties in the 1890s, two— the expansion of freedom of speech and the abolition of the unequal treaties with the Western powers—accorded with the maintenance of a common esprit for the parties. However, a third

---

[2] See my book, *Hara Kei in the Politics of Compromise* (Cambridge: Harvard University Press, 1967), and Peter Duus, *Party Rivalry in Taishō Japan* (Cambridge: Harvard University Press, 1968). Also Mitani Taichirō's excellent study, *Nihon seitōseiji no keisei* (Tokyo: Tokyo University Press, 1967); and Masumi, *Nihon seitōshi ron*, vol. 4. I have also written a short essay, "Inukai Tsuyoshi: Some Dilemmas in Party Development in Pre-World War II Japan," *The American Historical Review*, vol. 74 (December 1968): 492–510.

addressed itself to the specific grievance of the rural landed class, calling for the immediate reduction of the land tax. Concrete grievances of this kind could be easily manipulated by the ruling oligarchs to undermine the unity of the lower house. This situation called for a counterstrategy that would penetrate existing centers of constitutional power and redirect them from within to accord with the political interests of the lower house. In short, there developed a decided stress on a greater involvement in "politics" to satisfy specific economic interests, conceding that esprit alone could not maintain organizational discipline.

It was Hara Kei who perceived with great clarity the implications of the factional divisions of his day and intervened to give decisive direction to party politics in the early twentieth century. Hara was not a member of the oligarchy or a participant in the popular-rights movement and had sought a career in the bureaucracy, only to resign in 1892, along with Itō, in protest over the police interventions at the polls. He then became editor of a newspaper, the *Osaka Mainichi*, where his views on politics crystallized. He turned to party politics, becoming a growing influence in the Seiyūkai party under the aegis of Itō in 1900, then gaining leadership under the symbolic presidency of Saionji Kimmochi (1849–1940) until 1914, after which he himself assumed the presidency of that party.

The main elements in Hara's politics are easily discernible. Relying on Itō's prestige to legitimize the idea of party government, Hara publicly endorsed the view of balanced and functional constitutional politics and prepared himself and his party for a long and sustained struggle against the Yamagata faction and, more generally, those in government espousing the principle of government by a transcendent oligarchy. His actual aim, however, was not to achieve the "balance" Itō sought, but to transform the Seiyūkai into the most powerful political instrument within the constitutional system, a goal, needless to say, that was sharply opposed to the political views of the oligarchy.

Hara rejected the idea of an idealistic union among the parties, believing it to be untenable as a practical tactic. Espousing

· an uncompromising and ultimately revolutionary opposition (*daha*) while accepting the constitutional arrangements of power was a political contradiction: The parties must either choose total opposition or constitutional politics. Opting for the latter, Hara stressed the central importance of party discipline and loyalty, for which he believed the satisfaction of concrete interests of internal factions to be a necessary prerequisite. In short, he denied the practicality of an emotional union and emphasized the economic character of party organization.

Defining the dominant interest within his party by language such as "regional industrial development," which included the reduction of the land tax, Hara set forth between 1900 and 1920 to infiltrate the constitutional order, manipulate and weaken the Yamagata faction, and bend the system to satisfy the interests of party organization. Hara's tactic was to concede on certain demands, such as support for the government's budget, and to gain, in return, key appointments within the bureaucracy, notably in the home ministry that directed regional political and economic affairs through prefectural governors and key bureaus such as those of "regional affairs" and "public works." Hara's skill in continuously maintaining a relative bargaining advantage (primarily over Katsura Tarō [1847–1913], Yamagata's chief protégé), thereby assuring the unity and strength of his party, resulted in the steady decline of the Yamagata faction and the emergence of the Seiyūkai as the single most powerful political organization within the constitutional order.

Hara's impact on politics was extensive. He struck down Itō's ideal of constitutional government in which relatively equal constitutional bodies would be balanced harmoniously vis à vis each other; and he sharply redefined the oligarchy's conception of "loyal action" within fixed institutional confines to mean "partisan action," a fact that he justified with the rhetoric of Meiji loyalism, observing that partisan action was synonymous with loyal action for the nation as a whole. Needless to say, Hara's severest critics were those who did not subscribe to his equating of partisan politics with loyal activity. Within the party movement, moreover, Hara made it impossible to maintain an idealistic strategy to unify all of the parties into a single popular union. The idea itself persisted as an important ideology within the parties, especially since it harked back to the romantic years of the popular-rights movement. But, increasingly, political factions were compelled to orient themselves to the competitive acquisition of power and the immediate satisfaction of internal interests, eventually aligning themselves into two competitive and rival parties, one being Hara's Seiyūkai, the other being "anti-Seiyūkai," a basic pattern in Japanese party politics that has persisted down into the contemporary period.

Against the Seiyūkai there formed a rival coalition called Dōshikai in 1913, Kenseikai in 1915, and Minseitō after 1925. By whatever name it was called, its defining characteristic was its unity as an "anti-Seiyūkai" coalition. At various points, it included high-level bureaucrats identified with the oligarchs (Katsura Tarō and Ōura Kanetake [1850–1918], leaders from industry (Katō Kōmei [1860–1926]), and rising young bureaucrats (Hamaguchi Yūkō [1870–1931]). In contrast to the Seiyūkai, which traced its genealogy back to Itō and ultimately to the Jiyūtō of Itagaki, the anti-Seiyūkai coalition traced its origins to Itō's rival in the 1880s, Ōkuma and his party, the Kaishintō. As a multifactional coalition, it grew steadily in strength and in quality of leadership, competing with the Seiyūkai for power, and, by the mid-1920s, emerged under Katō and Hamaguchi as clearly the equal of the Seiyūkai and perhaps more effective and intelligent in its ability to seek out new legislation.

In their involvement in special-interest politics, however, the two parties were hardly distinguishable. Schools, dams, railroads and other projects for "regional industrial development" were built with government largesse and tied to partisan politics. In the central and prefectural bureaucracies and on down to the level of local hamlets the coercive mechanism of rival parties was felt. By 1918, when Hara assumed the prime ministership as the first "commoner" and party president in the lower house, there could be little doubt but that the character of constitutional politics had been dramatically reshaped. In 1900 the parties were on the fringes of the power structure; by 1918 they had become central in all of the major political relations within the constitutional order.

This changing balance in favor of political parties and the lower house was accompanied by a provocative reformulation of constitutional ideology that seemed to be in accord with the general political trend of the Taishō period (1912–26). Best articulated by Minobe Tatsukichi,[3] without question the best legal mind in prewar Japan, this ideology sanctioned the growth of representative institutions and of party government, and seemed, therefore, to reinforce the actual growth of party power. A dedicated scholar and professor of law at Tokyo University whose books on constitutional law were standard textbooks in all the universities, Minobe led a life quite different from that of a politician; yet, along with Hara, he played a crucial role in developing political change within the legal order.

Paralleling Hara's manipulation of constitutional politics, Minobe, relying on theoretical language from the German legal scholar Georg Jellinek (1851–1911), pointed the Japanese constitution in a liberal direction quite unintended by Itō and the other oligarchs who built the Meiji order. Although Minobe did not endorse pork-barrel politics, he shared with Hara an instrumentalist and utilitarian view of political institutions, or "organs" as he called them. Like Hara, he was not a critic of the constitu-

[3] A fine study of Minobe is Frank O. Miller, *Minobe Tatsukichi* (Berkeley: University of California Press, 1965). In Japanese: Ienaga Saburō, *Minobe Tatsukichi no shisōteki kenkyū* (Tokyo: Iwanami shoten, 1964); and Matsuo Takayoshi, *Taishō demokurashii no kenkyū* (Tokyo: Aoki shoten, 1966), pp. 238–74.

A recent essay by Sakai Yūkichi emphasizes Minobe's theoretical incorporation of "medieval constitutionalism," especially in regard to the Japanese monarchy, and revises the view that Minobe's rivals, such as Hozumi Yatsuka and Uesugi Shinkichi, were "traditionalists": "Meiji kempō to dentōteki kokkakan," in Ishii Shirō, ed., *Nihon kindai hōshi kōgi* (Tokyo: Seirin shoin, 1973), pp. 61–93.

tion. He emphasized, however, a redefinition of the actual content of constitutional government by proposing greater leeway in the functioning of constitutional bodies.

Minobe stated his case in the form of a defense of the Meiji constitutional order. The Meiji constitution, he argued, possessed an intrinsic "idea" common to all modern constitutional systems; and, although there were certain features peculiar to Japanese custom, notably the concept of inactive monarchy, it nonetheless defined Japan for the first time as a political system in a manner comparable to other modern states. A modern nation, he further elaborated, was a corporate society inclusive of all persons residing in it. It was this total corporate entity that is "sovereign": Its specific character was determined by "laws of organization" (*soshiki hō*), which defined and limited power; and each legal entity partook in the expression of sovereign will in ways defined by law. In the Meiji constitution, from the monarch at the top to the lowliest individual, all were part of the sovereign order. The monarchy alone was not sovereign but one among many "organs" of the nation, and it was explicitly limited by constitutional law. There was, furthermore, a Diet that legislated for the nation, and citizens (*kokumin*) were designated as elective instruments to select representatives to that legislative body. The "people," therefore, were also "organs" of the corporate order, and, as legal entities, were not merely passive recipients of political rule from above but actively contributed to shaping the course of politics. All modern constitutional systems, Minobe observed, included this dimension of limiting authority with law and of allowing a wide range of participation by members of society.

Minobe's ideas rested on a denial of the natural-right theory, and in this respect he fell within the tradition of political ideology shaped by Katō Hiroyuki and others a generation earlier. The source of law in this view was neither natural nor metaphysical but social and historical. Rights, therefore, did not inhere in human nature but, like sovereignty, were an extension of constitutional law and of contract. Each individual in society possessed a contract that defined his rights, including, in the Japanese case, access to public education, upward mobility based on demonstrated talent, the acquisition of wealth, the pursuit of self-development in diverse fields, and, in principle (although circumscribed in fact), participation in party and electoral politics. Unlike Katō, however, Minobe did not stress the virtue of selfless service within fixed constitutional structures but defined action within the constitution as an effort to express "reason" (rihō). In its most technical sense, "reason" was discovered through the scientific study of comparative law and the changing character of legal systems. As a practical matter, it was worked out in actual political, legislative, and electoral processes. It was in these processes, Minobe emphasized, that all constitutional systems underwent qualitative transformation. In short, the Meiji constitution was not fixed and unchanging since its content and meaning would inevitably change in its application and reapplication in history. The key to constitutional government, then, was how intelligent men actually made legal bodies function and adapt over time.

Minobe provided an important ideological synthesis for the twentieth century. He took the anti-natural-right position of Katō and gave it a decidedly "liberal" reading, allowing constitutional legitimization of vigorous and competitive politics as part and parcel of the formation and expression of constitutional "reason." Selfless loyalism was restated in the language of rational bureaucratic function and legal utility. Moreover, Minobe placed the Meiji constitution in comparative light, arguing for constitutionalism as essential to modern existence, thus denying the uniqueness of Japanese law. All constitutions, Minobe insisted, were governed by comparable principles: responsible and nonarbitrary government; popular participation; and a government responsive to social needs. At the same time, however, he conceded a link between the "written" Meiji constitution and the "unwritten" historical constitution of a symbolic and inactive monarchy. The idea of a national historical essence was not meaningless, he reasoned, for the monarchy continued to symbolize, as in the past, the shared feelings, beliefs, and historical memories of the national community, but this cultural fact should not be obscured with monarchical sovereignty in the legal sense. Minobe's synthesis combined in an impressive way both a comparative and a historical perception of constitutionalism, which he used to justify rational bureaucratic behavior and the greater power and influence of the lower house.

As the Taishō era advanced, it appeared that Minobe's ideas might attain preeminence in a field of contending ideologies and endure as a persuasive and empowering political orthodoxy for Japan. The presses and the universities sided overwhelmingly with Minobe in his debates with nationalistic pundits for imperial sovereignty, such as one of his colleagues at Tokyo University, Uesugi Shinkichi (1878–1929). And his major work of 1912 on constitutional theory, "Lectures on the Constitution" (*Kempō kōwa*; revised into final form in 1922), gained enormous fame as the textbook most widely used by faculties of constitutional law throughout the country. In 1932 he was appointed to a seat in the house of peers for his meritorious achievements as a legal scholar, a fact that epitomized acceptance and recognition of his stature by the established order itself.

It also appeared over these same years that the parties, beginning with the expansion of the Seiyūkai under Hara, would achieve undisputed political supremacy within the constitutional order. In 1918, Hara became prime minister of a party cabinet. As a "commoner" and as president of the powerful Seiyūkai in the lower house, Hara's prime ministership marked a new point in the history of Diet politics. In addition, a rival anti-Seiyūkai coalition emerged to challenge Hara and his party and, as part of opposition strategy, sponsored a vigorous movement for universal manhood suffrage. The movement was joined by the leading intellectuals, journalists, and publicists of the day. Identified with the movement were Yoshino Sakuzō (1878–1933), Fukuda Tokuzō, Miyake Setsurei (1860–1945), Ōyama Ikuo (1880–1956), Torii Sosen (1867–1928), and Hasegawa Nyozekan (1875–1969), unquestionably the leading intellectuals of the day. University students, especially at Tokyo University and Waseda University added a youthful and extremely vocal dimension to the movement. Labor unions such as Suzuki Bunji's (1885–1946) Yūaikai also took part, as did a women's voter rights contingency vigorously led by Hiratsuka Raichō (1886–) and Ichikawa Fusae (1893–). Under the prime ministership of Katō Kōmei, universal manhood suffrage was finally enacted in 1925, giving men above the age of twenty-five the right to vote. Although women were not extended the same right, universal manhood suffrage was viewed as a major political achievement within the Meiji constitutional order, providing dramatic evidence that the constitution was not static and that democratic reforms were indeed possible within its confines. Moreover, in the first general election of 1928, eight socialists were elected to the Diet (in 1936 the number increased to about twenty-two), not insignificant figures by any means when compared with previous election statistics, or, for that matter, with the relative achievements of other countries at about the same time. This again pointed to the possibility of substantive political reform and change within the guidelines of constitutional government.

Between 1918 and 1921, during Hara's prime ministership, and then again between 1924 and 1932, under the leadership of Katō Kōmei, Wakatsuki Reijirō (1866–1949), Hamaguchi Yūkō, and Inukai Tsuyoshi, the majority party in the lower house of the Diet dominated the cabinet and national politics. Party men gained enormous visibility in these years through their involvements in interparty rivalries, and this seemed to point to the clear ascendancy of party and parliamentary politics within the constitutional order, a matter some viewed as historically natural and inevitable in the course of modern development.

Yet, as is well known, these developments in Japan's constitutional thought and politics did not coalesce and hold firmly in place. The political world was staggered in 1921 with Hara's assassination by a ultrarightist in Tokyo Station. And in 1935, as we shall mention later, Minobe was rudely denounced in the house of peers for his constitutional theory. Large segments of the public were being influenced by ideas that made them look as-

kance at the partisan and instrumentalist conceptions of Hara and
Minobe, and these events pointed to a powerful undercurrent
of reaction against the rise of competitive partisan politics. While
no doubt providing hope to some, party politics created great
confusion and bitterness among bureaucrats, the military, and
intellectual leadership. For a nation whose security had barely
been achieved and whose cultural autonomy was still at issue,
partisan politics appeared an indefensible luxury, reflective of a
crass insensitivity to the wishes and needs of the people. Clearly,
pork-barrel politics was not what had been expected of industrial
development within the Meiji constitutional system, and this was
viewed as an irregularity that had to be rectified with what was
frequently termed the "normal course of constitutional government" (*kensei no jōdō*).

Although expressed through several different theoretical points
of view, all of the criticisms exhibit a comparable intellectual dis-
satisfaction with what was being achieved within the constitutional order. There was a pronounced popular and egalitarian
theme in the criticism of constitutional leadership: It was the
needs of the people as a whole that must be cared for, not the
interests of the special groups. Added to this was a concern, expressed often in strident and impatient language, over the waning
of moral idealism and spiritual vigor among the Japanese people
vis à vis the enormous expansion of industrial and governmental
bureaucracies and the need, therefore, for a new popular movement demanding social justice. Although these themes harked
back to patterns of thought developed in earlier periods, they assumed a theoretical content and character that were new, for
these concepts were not simply reiterated, but were consciously
refashioned to solve social and ethical questions that were distinctive to industrial Japan in the twentieth century.

POLITICAL CRITICISM IN TAISHŌ SOCIETY: POPULAR NATIONALISM, LIBERALISM, AND SOCIALISM

Much of early Taishō political criticism rested on a mode of
nationalist thought referred to variously as "Japanism," "people-

ism," and "national essentialism" (*Nihonshugi; minzokushugi; kokusuishugi*) first formulated in the 1890s by publicists such as Shiga Shigetaka (1863–1927), Miyake Setsurei, and Kuga Katsunan (1857–1907) and expanded in the 1920s by Nakano Seigō (1886–1943).[4] These men were harsh critics of the apparently mindless adulation of Western ideas and goods that appeared to captivate a good part of Japanese society, and, at the same time, they pointed out the failure of politics under the authoritarian bureaucratic rule of the oligarchs.

Their main contribution was the perception of nation, government, and emperor as popular institutions belonging to the people as a whole. The nation, they argued, was a moral community or a "people" made up of individuals with a capacity ("liberty" as this was sometimes expressed) to contribute in loyal and creative ways to the good of the entire society. For Miyake and Nakano each individual was endowed with a distinctive moral individuality, and the aim of politics was to unleash this power for social ends. There is here an obvious spiritual link with certain themes in the popular-rights movement. Saigō Takamori was invoked as the penultimate of spiritual independence and commitment. Itagaki Taisuke was also praised for his defense of liberty as were ideologues such as Ueki Emori. Both Miyake and Nakano went beyond Saigō to identify explicitly with the earlier Tokugawa moral idealism as formulated in the Ōyōmei tradition of Nakae Tōju and Kumazawa Banzan and as exemplified in the rebellious personality of Ōshio Heihachirō. As articulated by Nakano, the crucial significance of Ōshio and others in that tradition was their resistance to the imposition of corrupt politics and bureaucratic criteria on the people. Reminiscent of Ueki, moreover, Nakano insisted that moral resistance was a popular "right," a quality that all persons in Japan possessed and could be reminded of by recalling great historical figures such as

---

[4] These figures are discussed in Kenneth B. Pyle, *The New Generation in Meiji Japan* (Stanford: Stanford University Press, 1969). I have written "Nakano Seigō and the Spirit of the Meiji Restoration in Twentieth-Century Japan," in James Morley, ed., *Dilemmas of Growth in Prewar Japan* (Princeton: Princeton University Press, 1971), pp. 375–421.

Ōshio, Saigō, and Itagaki. Like these activists, all ought to participate vigorously in the politics of resistance to the spread of bureaucratism.

The real link between the popular nationalism of Japan early in the twentieth century and the popular-rights movement in Meiji, then, was in a shared skepticism about bureaucratic government and not in a common commitment to a natural-right theory. What was being idealized was a spirit of moral individualism that was believed to define something precious and distinctive about the Japanese people and their national history. In this respect, the underlying premise of popular nationalism was reminiscent of Katō Hiroyuki and his "anti-natural-right" position. Katō, it will be recalled, stressed that society was a moral community whose integrating spiritual values were derived from history and were not, a priori, of nature. Katō, however, relied on this theory to affirm the necessity of constitutional bureaucracy to regulate and order the evolution of Japan into a great and independent nation; and Minobe expanded on this theory and turned it toward a justification of constitutionalism as the progressive search for an exercise of legal reason. The advocates of popular nationalism, on the other hand, used the same premise to emphasize the fundamental contradiction between bureaucratism and the creative idealism of the Japanese people. Like Minobe, they supported wider popular participation in politics, but for idealistic reasons and not because individuals were legal "instruments" in the sovereign order. Thus, while in theory they sided with Katō and Minobe, their emotional identifications were with the spirit of resistance found in the popular-rights movement and with the articulate and rebellious loyalism of late Tokugawa society.

Bureaucratic instruments were important insofar as they enhanced the spiritual well-being of the people as a whole, an objective sometimes described as "national socialism" or the realization of the shared ideals of "truth, goodness, and beauty" (*shinzenbi*).[5] The point was that everyone, not just men of high

5 The phrase is from a book by Miyake Setsurei, *Shinzenbi Nihonjin* published in 1891 on the ideal values in Japanese history. Among other places,

status, had a historical and social "right" to share in the spiritual and aesthetic values of the national community, and hence also to enjoy the concrete fruits of governmental action. The government, these men concluded, belonged to the people, not the oligarchs, and the people must determine and shape their common destiny (shimei).

In a similar vein, the emperor was defined as a popular and aesthetic institution. As a symbol of a continuous social history, the emperor linked an aesthetic past with the present by giving life to extraordinary moments of creation in the past that confirmed the creative potential of everyone in the present. Beginning in late Meiji, great creative expressions locked in temples, rock gardens, religious sculpture, scrolls, and literary anthologies were designated "national cultural treasures" and protected with meticulous care. The emperor as a god-king was made to represent pure human potential in the continuing history of the nation and to strengthen the Japanese cultural and aesthetic self-image. Most important, the emperor was redefined from a distant religious figure to a popular institution, a constant spiritual presence accessible to and, indeed, spiritually coincidental with everyone. This idea carried with it strong political significance. The emperor did not belong to a few powerful men; he was "the people's emperor" (kokumin no tennō), and the constitutional system over which he reigned likewise should belong to the people and function according to popular participation.

This concept of an autonomous popular culture defined by distinctive historical values and leading, through popular participation, to a common destiny, carried with it an obvious "pan-Asian" dimension. The argument that the West ought not to be uncritically emulated spilled over into an articulate plea, for example by Okakura Tenshin (1862–1913), that Japan ought to "return to Asia" (Nyū-A), to that cultural zone within which

---

it is included in Kanō Masanao, ed., Nihon no meicho, vol. 37, Kuga Katsunan, Miyake Setsurei (Tokyo: Chūōkōronsha, 1971), pp. 283–324. A suggestive piece is Takeda Kiyoko, "Kakumei shisō to tennōsei," in Hashikawa Bunzō and Matsumoto Sannosuke, eds., Kindai Nihon seiji shisōshi, vol. 2, pp. 252–300.

Japan had developed historically as an independent nation and in which Japan's true concerns and proper responsibilities ought to lie.[6] According to this view, all societies within a cultural zone shared certain spiritual themes in common, but each also developed distinctive creative characteristics. More specifically all Asian nations had a cultural right to realize their own distinctive and creative potential within an Asian context, with minimal interference from the West. Because it had successfully resisted the West, it was Japan's responsibility to maintain itself as a strong and defiant model of Asian independence in a competitive modern world dominated by Western power. The thought behind this line of reasoning was cultural, but, needless to say, it could be easily reworked (as it was in the late 1930s) to justify the expansionist "liberation of Asia" by Japan.

The importance of popular nationalism in Taishō political criticism, however, lay in its sustained plea for popular participation in parliamentary government. The underlying rationale was not that parliamentary forms were thought best suited to accommodate interest groups. It was a spiritual and moral plea and had a telling effect on political opinion. Especially influential were the demand that all artificial barriers standing between the people and emperor be dismantled and the related charge against the oligarchs, and the Yamagata faction in particular, of arbitrary rule, spiritual poverty, and bureaucratic insensitivity in dealing with the political and cultural affairs of the nation. It was this voice of popular nationalism that contributed greatly to undermining the public's image of the oligarchs and the privileged in the house of peers. It is a fact of modern Japanese politics that despite their close proximity to imperial charisma, the oligarchs were viewed with great distrust and held in extremely low esteem, neither receiving nor transferring the heroic splendor which the emperor embodied for the people. Yamagata Aritomo's death in 1922 was hardly mourned by the public.

[6] On the idea of a national destiny, see Matsumoto Sannosuke, *Kindai no seiji to ningen*, pp. 199–255. Available in English is Okakura Tenshin, *Ideals of the East* (Rutland: Tuttle, 1970; first published in London, 1902).

Equally important, through its criticism of the oligarchs and bureaucratic elitism, popular nationalism converged with other voices of protest in the Taishō period, notably those of liberal democracy and socialism, both essentially nonnationalistic modes of thinking. The conceptual premises of these schemes of thought were far more cosmopolitan, far less "Asian," in vocabularly and theory. Yet there is a common strain of populist and egalitarian thinking, a strong romantic identification with the emotional and spiritual needs of the people, and a powerful antipathy for the bureaucratic and political elites ensconced in the constitutional order.

The pivotal figure bridging popular nationalist thought and liberal criticism was Yoshino Sakuzō,[7] a professor in the faculty of law at Tokyo University, and, without question, the most prominent publicist of the Taishō era. A Christian humanist, Yoshino employed the language of idealistic liberalism then current in the West and stood at the forefront of reform movements such as universal suffrage. Yoshino retained the populist spirit as well as the idealization of individual moral autonomy emphasized in popular nationalist thought. In the mid-1900s he began advocating "government based on the people" (mimponshugi), which eventually turned into a movement for moral and spiritual as well as political reform.

Yoshino pointed to mass demonstrations in late Meiji as historical evidence of the steady growth of popular political consciousness. The people were becoming aware of the contradiction between inner ideals and politics and had begun to "objectify" their ethical wishes on existing politics through direct movements of protest. These wishes, he further reasoned, could be channeled

[7] Mitani Taichirō, ed., Nihon no meicho, vol. 48, Yoshino Sakuzō (Tokyo: Chūōkōronsha, 1972), especially Mitani's introductory essay, pp. 7–62. A useful biography is Tanaka Sōgorō, Yoshino Sakuzō (Tokyo: Miraisha, 1958). I have written "Some Reflections on Idealism in the Political Thought of Yoshino Sakuzō," which will appear in a volume edited by Harry D. Harootunian and Bernard Silberman on Taishō politics and society to be published by Princeton University Press; and Henry D. Smith has recently published Japan's First Student Radicals (Cambridge: Harvard University Press, 1972).

through universal suffrage and responsible parliamentary government, both attainable under the existing constitutional framework. And, despite the existence of elite groups (oligarchs, bureaucratic cliques, house of peers, and military factions) working in his interest, the emperor actually harbored feelings that were theoretically and ethically identical with the wishes of the people. Thus, although the Japanese constitutional order was "monarchical" in design, it could be transformed into a democratic and popular system of governance. What Yoshino wished to emphasize was that constitutional bodies, including the imperial institution, were not static edifices but embodiments of human values and expectations. It was imperative, however, that men develop a "new consciousness" or become "new men" (*shinjin*, a name he used for the political association he organized in 1918) to reshape existing institutions in the image of that consciousness. Political progress, then, involved a constant redefinition of institutions in accordance with human enlightenment. The greater the number of "new men" involved in politics, the greater the potential for enlightened reform.

Like Minobe Tatsukichi, Yoshino accepted the constitution. It could be reformed from within to accord with democratic theory and enlightened social opinion. Minobe's constitutional theory, however, emphasized the rationality of governmental performance and therefore legitimated specialized bureaucratic elites. Individuals, for Minobe, should participate in politics as "instruments" of the constitutional system; thus there could be little doubt but that the political individual was always conceptualized within a hierarchy of power since some institutions were obviously more important and powerful than others. Yoshino, however, was an "idealist," not an "instrumentalist." He concerned himself with the moral potential of the individual to reshape politics into what ideally it ought to be (*arubeki seiji*). Thus, while Minobe's writings served as a handbook for aspiring bureaucrats, Yoshino's served as an incentive for a critical intelligentsia in the late 1910s and 1920s.

Yoshino's significance increased in this regard as prospects for fundamental political improvement began to appear doubtful. Factional strife dominated politics; the enactment of universal manhood suffrage in 1925 did not result in a new consciousness but in the expansion of special-interest politics; and a "peace-preservation law" was enacted, also in 1925, to curb radical political criticism. All of these developments tended to confirm the view that politics had become irretrievably corrupt. Accepting this assessment, Yoshino increasingly emphasized the ethical principle of total moral freedom from existing political organization, a view sometimes characterized as "personalism" or as "Neo-Kantianism."

Yoshino's ideas were potentially antipolitical. Yoshino himself did not take his thought to a militant conclusion, consistently abhorring the implications of a total political rejection of the present. His colleagues and many of his students, however, felt otherwise and sought to break out of the restraints of liberal criticism. Yoshino's humanitarian values and his insistence on moral autonomy were not being challenged. It was rather the conception of social creation through individual consciousness that increasingly appeared ineffective as a prescription for action, for in this theoretical scheme, the "individual" and "political society" must continuously interact to evolve a better future. This evolutionary perspective seemed flawed, however, since the individual was at a severe disadvantage, constantly being coerced by the wider political system without fully understanding the fundamental character of those structures. What seemed to be required was a new basis of objectivity, a new perspective to explain precisely what conscious individuals must confront; and in this regard, the crucial intellectual outlet from liberal criticism was provided by the Marxist theory of history and social structure.

What Marxism provided was a conceptual system that gave more explicit and cogent expression to already existing feelings of moral indignation about constitutional politics and the general failings of modernization. Perhaps the most influential Marxist writer in the 1920s among young Japanese intellectuals and Chinese students in Japan was Kawakami Hajime (1879–1946).[8] Kawakami's discomfort with modernity clearly preceded his adoption of Marxist theory. Rejecting the concept of self-interest and utility as inadequate for modern life, Kawakami joined, in the early 1910s, a movement to spread the principle of "selfless love" (*muga ai*), the ideal drawn from the Buddhist tradition (from Zen and Faith Buddhism in Kawakami's case) to help the poverty-stricken and the lowly. From this religious perspective, he wrote a famous serial in the newspaper *Osaka Asahi* in 1916 called "Tales of Poverty" (*Bimbō monogatari*), certainly one of the classics in the development of socialist thought in Taishō Japan. In this account, Kawakami outlined his reasons for viewing modernity, and economic modernity in particular, as a failure. The expansion of industrial wealth had also produced unprecedented poverty and in this sense poverty itself was a "modern" phenomenon and the greatest malaise of all industrial nations, including those of the West and Japan itself. The flaw of modernity, Kawakami elaborated, was its ethic of self-aggrandizement, the view that the pursuit of wealth at the expense of others is somehow a "natural," "scientific," and cosmic "principle." It was this ethical perception that steered Kawakami to Marxism and, in 1919, he began writing a guidebook to and translation of Marx's *Das Kapital*.

It is important to note that throughout the remainder of his turbulent career (including five years' imprisonment from 1933 to 1937), Kawakami continued to believe deeply in the principle of "selfless love." Not a mere opiate or "philosophy," as it might be described within Marxist theory, the Buddhist ethic of selfless-

---

[8] Some of Kawakami's writings are collected in Ōuchi Hyōei, ed., *Gendai Nihon shisō taikei*, vol. 19, *Kawakami Hajime* (Tokyo: Chikuma shobō, 1964). See especially "Mugaen no jidai," pp. 138–61; and "Bimbō monogatari," pp. 165–267. See also Tsunoda, de Bary, and Keene, eds., *Sources of the Japanese Tradition*, pp. 820–27 and 872–80. For a discussion of the critique of Ōsugi Sakae, Ōyama Ikuo, and others on Yoshino, see Matsumoto and Hashikawa, eds., *Kindai Nihon seiji shisōshi*, vol. 2, pp. 173–86.

ness accorded with the modern Marxist idea of objective action, Kawakami insisted, because it showed a conscious potential in men to act entirely for the good of others, a conception of action that social theory did not clarify. But religious conviction did not explain how one should act in his own time and, more importantly, against what kinds of social reality. This could only be understood through a detailed and "scientific" exposition of objective social history and political structure. Kawakami's theory of action, in short, derived in good measure from indigenous ideas (a fact that explains his identification with Yoshida Shōin as a hero in history), while Marxism provided him with the explanatory construction through which to perceive the arena and structure of politics and allow for a necessary intellectual disengagement from the flow of national history.

The search for a scientific characterization of modern Japan, however, turned out to be an exceedingly difficult and time-consuming task. It captured the attention of an entire generation of scholars and university students, and their debates and scholarly writings created a distinctive esprit that has had a deep and lasting influence on Japanese intellectual life. To begin with, the evolutionary view of history was denounced as a compilation of descriptive accounts that confirmed the present as a comprehensive outgrowth of the past, a history leading from primitive and medieval to an industrial and rational modern nation. Such a view, however, glossed over the relationship between the creation of wealth and the existence of social classes, in particular the systematic deprivation of the masses. Through the dialectical method of Marxism, the contrasting and contradictory realities in history of affluence and anguished poverty could be seen in clear analytical light and be shown to be a continuing contradiction in the historical present.

More concretely, this general view was applied to systematic historical studies that rejected Japan's modernity in sweeping and unequivocal language. The mainstream of these studies came to be called the "Lecture School" (Kōza ha), a name taken from the title of volumes of researched "lectures" on Japanese capitalism[9] and identified with scholars such as Noro Eitarō (1900–1934), the key inspirational figure, Hani Gorō (1901–), Yamada Moritarō (1897–), Hirano Yoshitarō (1897–), Hattori Shisō (1901–56), and others, all of whom have been extremely well-known figures in Japanese intellectual life.

First outlined by Noro Eitarō, the arguments of this group were based on the following historical scheme. The basic contradiction of Japanese feudalism was the status deprivation of talented lower *samurai* and merchants who had accumulated vast amounts of wealth in the course of the Tokugawa period. This contradiction was ostensibly resolved, through the leadership of the lower *samurai* especially, in the Meiji Restoration, the crucial event dividing preindustrial from industrial Japan. Due in part to the impingement of Western imperialism, however, the new regime relied on a collusion of contradictory forces, an alliance of reactionary feudal elements (the emperor, court nobles, high-ranking former *samurai*, and especially landlords) and new industrialists and intellectual leaders. The resulting semifeudal mode of industrialization explains the curious "absolutism" of the twentieth century. Beneath all this jargon was the harsh emotional and intellectual judgment that the Meiji Restoration was an incomplete and inadequate event and that while Japan had industrialized, its modernity was abortive and dehumanizing for the people.

This interpretation tended to prevail as the orthodox Marxist overview of modern Japanese history. A rival position, the "Labor-Farmer School" (*Rōnō-ha*),[10] formulated by scholars such as

[9] Noro Eitarō et al., eds., *Nihon shihonshugi hattatsushi kōza*, 7 vols. (Tokyo: Iwanami shoten, 1932–33). The pilot work for this set of volumes was Noro's *Nihon shihonshugi hattatsushi* (Tokyo: Tettō shoin, 1930).

[10] One of the lasting contributions of the Rōnō faction is the uncovering of vast amounts of new historical data as in Ōuchi Hyoei and Tsuchiya Takao, *Meiji zenki zaisei keizai shiryō shūsei*, 12 vols. (Tokyo: Kaizōsha, 1931–36). A useful work is Tsuchiya Takao, *Nihon shihonshugishi ronshū* (Tokyo: Kaizōsha, 1937).

A discussion of both Rōnō and Kōza schools is found in Kitayama Shigeo,

Tsuchiya Takao (1896–) and Ōuchi Hyōei (1888–), challenged
the Lecture School with the view that the Meiji Restoration was
a "bourgeois revolution" and not an abortive event. The land-
lord class, however anachronistic its ideology, was a modern class
since it was a peasantry in the previous feudal era; and the relationship between feudal elements and capitalists was not at all
a true alliance but at best an extremely unequal partnership, with
the industrial class clearly possessing the upper and manipulative
hand. In short, the imperial system was fundamentally "bourgeois," dominated by monopoly capitalism rather than by feudal
forces. Despite this strong minority view, however, it was the interpretation of the Lecture School that had the greater influence.

Its special strength was that it could explain cogently, more
so than other interpretive schemes, the persistence in the twentieth century of social misery that seemed unusual and extreme.
Had the Restoration been a more thoroughgoing revolution, it
was argued, there would not have been the curious fusion of
feudal and industrial forces but rather a society resembling a
liberal and democratic order. Although oppressive in certain ways,
such an order would clearly not resemble the absolutism that confronted the Japanese. A comparative perspective was also brought
into focus, showing Japan to be less like Great Britain and France,
the liberal democratic models of the West, and more like Russia
prior to the Revolution of 1917 in the mix of monarchy, land-
lordism, and industrialism (a view affirmed by the Comintern
theses of 1927 and 1932 in regard to Japan). Such a comparison
gave hope for a revolutionary breakthrough in Japan as had been
achieved in Russia, thus reinforcing the agitation for militant
protest against the legal order.

Clearly, Marxist social theory provided an important concep-

"Nihon kindai shigaku no hattatsu," *Iwanami kōza, Nihon rekishi*, vol. 22
(Tokyo: Iwanami shoten, 1963), pp. 105–63. The Rōnō group tended to
publish in the journal *Rōnō*. The emphasis was on the domination of the
bourgeoisie over both workers (*rō*) and farmers (*nō*). Perhaps the best statement on this position is Yamakawa Hitoshi, *Tan'itsu musan seitō ron* (Tokyo:
Bungei sensen shuppanbu, 1930).

tual platform outside the evolution of national history from which to criticize politics and allow intellectual independence and integrity. Kawakami, Noro, Hani, and others were not mere puppets of the Comintern, as has sometimes been suggested, but men who struggled to maintain the freedom of the universities from bureaucratic interference and to support a general resistance to the direction that Japanese history had taken. Indeed, the best of them were intellectuals and publicists with broad cosmopolitan interests. One cannot but be impressed, for example, with the range of Hani's writings, which cover such topics as "Asian capitalism" in China, India, and Japan; Arai Hakuseki, the eighteenth-century Tokugawa rational thinker; and Michelangelo.[11] Most of all, however, Marxism provided a theory of total intellectual and political disengagement from the present on the ground that history had gone wrong. This Marxist view of history in time came to be shared by many of the intellectual and university strata of the 1920s, although the majority did not become underground revolutionaries, as did Kawakami and Noro, choosing instead to assume a distant disengagement from politics. Thus, while leading critics of the Meiji era had discussed why a "constitution" was desirable and why, even if imperfect in design, a constitution might be made to perform in a humane and liberating manner, critics of the mid-Taishō years came around to the view that perhaps the existing constitutional order had failed and could not be made to work as previously believed. And in this regard, idealistic liberals in Yoshino's tradition and socialists in Kawakami's were often in substantial accord.

In short, the optimism of Meiji regarding the future of constitutional government had deteriorated seriously by the mid-1920s. The possibility of a rally for existing politics seemed dim as an allegiance of the politically articulate class seemed dissipated

---

11 For example, Hani Gorō, *Hakuseki, Yukichi* (Tokyo: Iwanami shoten, 1937); "Mikuruanjero no Pieta," *Bōsei* (April 1941); and *Meiji Ishin shi kenkyū* (Tokyo: Iwanami shoten, 1956). His various essays have been collected in *Hani Gorō rekishiron chosakushū*, 4 vols. (Tokyo: Aoki shoten, 1967).

in intellectual commitments that were not aimed at providing empowering support for constitutional rule. Adding to this declining sense of certainty about the effectiveness of politics was the mounting criticism from another more virulent and action-oriented point of view, namely that of radical restorationism.

The 1930s would witness a restorationist revolt against interest politics and the industrial and bureaucratic elitism enmeshed in the constitutional system. The central criticism was directed against the leadership's failure to achieve the socially just and strategically powerful nation envisioned in the Meiji Restoration. Some of the ideas of the new restorationism overlapped with the thought of popular nationalism discussed earlier. But its real inspiration was the thought and movement for restoration in late Tokugawa, to which was added political ideas distinctive to modern Japan. Although referred to in composite form as the "Shōwa Restoration," it was not a single event involving actors espousing identical political ideas and formulae for action. It was, more basically, a series of radical criticisms based on idealistic and utilitarian perceptions of politics identifiable with the Japanese tradition of restorationism. This restoration movement did not take power in a clear and unequivocal way, as was the case in the 1860s, but it nonetheless disrupted constitutional politics and put to a severe test the self-confidence of the political leadership. While intellectuals of the Left could be hounded, harassed, and suppressed, those advocating radical restorationism could not easily be treated with impunity, it being public knowledge that their loyalty to the emperor and nation was impeccable and that military men ensconced in high positions within the established order itself shared some of their discontents.

RESTORATIONISM IN THE TWENTIETH CENTURY

As with its historical prototype in late Tokugawa, twentieth-century restorationism combined two distinguishable perceptions of history: idealism and a pragmatic, utilitarian view of politics and national strategy. Restorationists were at times diametrically opposed, especially as manifested in the much-discussed military factions, the action-oriented "Imperial Way Faction" (Kōdō ha), and the pragmatic "Control Faction" (Tōsei ha).[12] They were unified, however, in their belief that the goals envisaged in the Meiji Restoration that would have maintained national integrity and expansive autonomy (jōi, as rendered in late Tokugawa) and achieved social justice at home for the oppressed people never reached maturity within constitutional government. Either perception could involve a radical rejection of the political present and, through a variety of tactics, demand a new arrangement of power.

A number of events are easily identified with the reemergence of strident restorationism. With the start of World War I, a general discussion arose regarding the logistical capacity of the Japanese political system in the event of a total war. As elsewhere at this time, the view was publicized that future conflicts would no longer be quick and decisive affairs but wars of attrition in which total and final victory would go to the better-mobilized and spiritually and logistically more powerful political system. Added to this discussion was the contention that such a war with the West was inevitable, a view documented later at the meetings at Versailles, where it appeared certain the West would not relinquish its domination over Asia. Subsequent events such as the Washington and London naval conferences of 1921–1922 and 1930 (in which Great Britain and the United States seemed clearly aligned against Japan), the exclusion of Japanese immigrants by the United States in 1924, and the growth of mechanized Soviet power on the Asian continent all confirmed the early concern of an impending confrontation with the West. It would be the war to end all wars (saishū sensō).

From the mid-1920s on into the 1930s the demand for a sec-

---

[12] A discussion of military politics in regard to Japanese diplomacy is James B. Crowley, *Japan's Quest for Autonomy* (Princeton: Princeton University Press, 1966), pp. 244–300. See also Itō Takashi, *Shōwa shoki seijishi kenkyū* (Tokyo: Tokyo daigaku shuppankai, 1969) pp. 283–324 and Takahashi Masae, *Showa no gumbatsu* (Tokyo: Chuōkoronsha, 1969).

ond revolutionary restoration, a "Shōwa Restoration," became increasingly vocal. On both land and sea, it was argued, the government had capitulated to the West, conceding unfavorable tonnage ratios at the naval conferences and reducing the size of the army (in 1922), to weaken Japan's stance against Soviet Russia on the Asian continent. Singled out for criticism were Diet and party politicians and, particularly after the Great Depression of 1929, leaders of high finance and industry as well.

In the forefront of this criticism were young officers and nationalistic civilians closely identified with a group of military men called the Imperial Way Faction. Armed with militant nationalist ideas, these men resorted to direct action and terrorism in the early 1930s, introducing a level of violence resembling that in Kyoto in the early 1860s on the eve of the Meiji Restoration. They were inspired by ideas directly traceable to the new ideologues of restorationism such as Tachibana Kōsaburō (1893–), Gondō Seikei (1868–1937), Inoue Nisshō (1886–1967), and, especially, Kita Ikki (1883–1937).[13]

Several common themes are readily discernible in these thinkers. There was an insistence on religious commitment, the reliance on faith in a traditional belief, as, for example, in the idealistic intuitionism of Inoue, the ancient agrarian communalism of Tachibana, and the Lotus Sutra in Kita. "Action" was finally pinned to a faith outside of the present and in the past, a matter deemed essential for disengagement from present politics and for total radical commitment. All appealed to the individual's capacity for self-sacrifice against insurmountable opposition, against the powerful establishment itself; in short, to stand for one's belief unto death (*shi o motte tate*, in the language of Tachibana).

---

[13] Key essays of Tachibana, Gondō, Inoue, Kita, and others are reprinted in Imai Seiichi and Takahashi Masae, eds., *Gendaishi shiryō*, vol. 4, *Kokkashugi undō* (Tokyo: Misuzu shobō, 1963); and Hashikawa Bunzō, ed., *Gendai Nihon shisō taikei*, vol. 31, *Chōkokkashugi* (Tokyo: Chikuma shobō, 1964). See also Kunō Osamu and Tsurumi Shunsuke, *Gendai Nihon no shisō* (Tokyo: Iwanami shoten, 1956); and Matsuzawa Tetsunari, *Tachibana Kōsaburō* (Tokyo: Sanichi shobō 1972). A good general coverage is in Matsumoto and Hashikawa, eds., *Kindai Nihon seiji shisōshi*, vol. 2, pp. 209–300.

There was, moreover, a tendency to define political objectives in terms of egalitarian populism or socialism within the national framework. Connected with this was a fierce identification with the physical environment, an intense sense of the "native land" (*kokudo*). Tachibana's basic reasoning, therefore, proceeded in this manner: There is no "people" apart from the "native land"; there is no "national society" without a "people"; without a "national society" there is no real "human life"; but the possession of all these means that all members of society, and hence in all of Japan, are "brothers" (*dōhō*), sharing common feelings, fears, aspirations, and utterly equal before one another.[14]

All these new "restorationists" were convinced that the nation was in a state of crisis from which it must be "saved." From their view, however, the real cause of the crisis was not so much the foreign powers but the enemies of the people *within* Japan. Thus, they pointed to the bureaucratic elites, the large industrial combines or *zaibatsu*, and special-interest and partisan politics as the root causes of the existing crisis. For some of them, as in the case of Gondō, the critique was directed explicitly against Itō's view of constitutionalism which, in the final analysis, was thought to have suppressed popular opinion and allowed the rise of self-centered elites. When these men spoke of "restoration," then, they meant a total reconstruction of the domestic order to liberate the people at home (*kokumin kaihō*).

The most influential theorist by far was Kita Ikki,[15] whose ideas are agreed to have been central to the Shōwa Restoration. A complex thinker and personality, Kita placed a mystical faith

[14] Tachibana, "Nihon aikoku kakushin hongi," in Hashikawa, ed., *Chōkokkashugi*, pp. 213–39.

[15] Kita's two most famous essays are his early statement of 1906 on "pure socialism," "Kokutai oyobi junsei shakaishugi," which is reproduced as the first volume of his collected works, *Kita Ikki chosakushū*, 3 vols. (Tokyo: Misuzu shobō, 1959); and his outline for national reconstruction, "Nihon kaizō hōan taikō," published in 1919, and included in Hashikawa, ed., *Chōkokkashugi*, pp. 283–347. In English: George M. Wilson, *Radical Nationalist in Japan: Kita Ikki, 1883–1937* (Cambridge: Harvard University Press, 1969).

in the Lotus Sutra to sustain his revolutionary commitments; but he also combined this religiosity with radical socialist ideas that defined his political objectives. Kita's interest in a socialist revolution began in the early 1900s while he was a student at Waseda University. In Tokyo he frequented the meetings of the Tung Meng Hui, which was a group of revolutionary Chinese activists committed to the overthrow of the old imperial order. Kita befriended its members and finally joined its ranks in the Chinese Revolution of 1911. His writings of these years attracted a great deal of attention in the Japanese underground and are said to have been as widely read as the Communist Manifesto itself.

Kita's theory of revolutionary action was predicated on the belief that the highest ideal toward which the Japanese should aspire was socialism, or, in his words, "pure socialism" (*junsei shakaishugi*). It was an ideal that coincided with the nation's historical essence, which the monarchy had been made to symbolize. Not to be confused with sovereignty, the monarchy represented the entire people and therefore also the highest social ideal that a people has of itself, an order that was just and without special social and economic privilege and exploitation.

In Asia such an order of social justice could not be achieved through the much discussed Western pattern of class struggle. The powerful impingement of Western imperialism dictated revolutionary popular and national struggles (*minzokukyōsō kokkakyōsō*) in which class identifications must be replaced with the cause of national unity and autonomy. In Japan's case, the Meiji Restoration had made such a transformation possible leading to the defeat of a Western nation in the Russo-Japanese War of 1905, an event, according to Kita, that triggered movements for independence in China and India and remained fundamental to the Japanese legacy of militant resistance to the West. The Meiji Restoration, however, was flawed in certain respects. Although a political revolution in the sense that it established the principle of legal equality among Japanese citizens, it was finally articulated in a constitutional settlement that used the monarchy to buttress bureaucratic and industrial elitism. This contradicted the spirit of the nation, thus necessitating another revolution, or "restorationist revolution," as he called it, to end both economic privelege and poverty and to build a new order of popular justice. Without such a revolution, warned Kita, Japan would not survive the new efforts of the West to dominate Asia: Japan, therefore, must choose between "revolution or national ruin" (*kakumei ka bōkoku ka*).

These views were sketched out in Kita's blueprint for revolution, "A General Outline for National Reconstruction" (*Nihon kaizō hōan taikō*). Written in Shanghai in 1919, it was smuggled into Japan and banned by the government, but published twice nonetheless with certain terms left unprinted. Although Kita's new order cannot be detailed here, it is important to observe that he called for wide-ranging structural changes, including destruction of the house of peers, the privy council, the imperial household, the *zaibatsu*, and all wealthy households above a stipulated level of wealth; censorship and peace preservation codes would be abolished; and universal suffrage and equality before the law would be guaranteed to everyone.

What impressed radical activists and young officers especially were Kita's socialist ideas combined with the belief in the inevitability of an ultimate confrontation with the West, which necessitated immediate and uncompromising action in the present. For Kita, terror and revolt were legitimate means to break the power of the entrenched constitutional elites and to establish a new order of socialism that would be powerful enough to expel the West from Asia. It was this plea for immediate revolt against domestic politics that decisively influenced ultranationalists such as Nishida Zei (1901–37), a leading devotee of Kita, and a host of lesser-known young officers (such as Gotō Eihan, Isobe Asakichi, Muranaka Kōji, and others) to carry out a reign of terror and assassination in the early 1930s.

Between 1930 and 1936 key figures in the constitutional elite were struck down: Hamaguchi Yūkō and Inoue Junnosuke (November 2, 1930); Inukai Tsuyoshi (May 15, 1932); Saitō Makoto and Takahashi Korekiyo (February 26, 1936). A dozen others were hunted and harassed, and some of them were seriously wounded. All these men were strategic figures in the cabinet, Diet, and in high finance and industry. The death of Hamaguchi was especially significant. A dominant figure in the Minseitō, one of the leading parties in the Diet, Hamaguchi had defied the military and gained parliamentary endorsement of the London Naval Treaty in 1930. Like Hara of the rival Seiyūkai (also a victim of assassination ten years earlier), Hamaguchi was committed to the principle of civilian control over the military. His death left the political leadership in a state of disarray from which it did not fully recover.[16]

The culmination of violent revolt came in the so-called February 26 Incident of 1936. In this, the most elaborate of their plots, the rebels, totalling some 1,400 troops, captured the center portion of Tokyo and hunted down members of the cabinet and imperial household. Expected support from key generals Mazaki Jinzaburō (1876–1956) and Araki Sadao (1877–), was not forthcoming however, so that, reminiscent of the attack on the Forbidden Gate in 1864, the revolt was abortive. It collapsed after two days, and eighteen of the leaders were subsequently executed (including Kita Ikki himself, who allegedly offered advice to the rebels by phone). Like the Incident at the Forbidden Gate, however, this event in 1936, as a culmination of a dozen other acts of terror and assassination, severely undermined the political stability of the time. Key cabinet-level leaders were killed, stimulating others presumably committed to the constitutional center to move toward "reconstructionist" positions, and, in general, generating a shift in the character of the political coalitions within the legal

16 The view sometimes advanced that politics basically went on as usual in the 1930s no longer appears tenable in the light of the recent work of Itō Takashi, Shōwa shoki seijishi kenkyū, mentioned in note 12 above. In this impressively documented study, Itō discusses the impact of radical nationalism on Shōwa politics and on the movement for a "new structure" and "new party." See also Itō's "Kyokoku itchi naikaku ki no seikai hensei mondai," Shakaikagaku kenkyū 24, no. 1 (1972): 56–130. See also Richard Storry, The Double Patriots (Boston: Houghton Mifflin Company, 1957); and the recent study by Ben-Ami Shillony, "The February 26 Affair: Politics of a Military Insurrection," in George M. Wilson, ed., Crisis Politics in Prewar Japan (Tokyo: Sophia University Press, 1970), pp. 25–50.

order, allowing in particular the ascendency of a military group
known as the "Control Faction" to assume great power.

The Control Faction[17] was formed early in the 1930s and included activists such as Hashimoto Kingorō (1897–1957) and
other young officers of the so-called Cherry Blossom Society,
which plotted violent coups d'état to establish military control of
the government. Under its principal leader, General Nagata Tet-
suzan (1884–1935), however, terrorist plots were rejected in favor of a ruthlessly pragmatic course of action, the manipulation
of political institutions and formation of convenient alliances with
expansion-minded industrialists and bureaucratic factions, known
variously as "new bureaucrats" and "reform bureaucrats," to
achieve the ultimate end of total national mobilization under the
aegis of the military. Resistance to this view of tactics by young
activists was extremely fierce in the mid-1930s, however, and in a
highly publicized incident (August 14, 1935), Colonel Aizawa Saburō, claiming to carry out "heaven's will" (tenchū), brutally assassinated General Nagata in his chief of staff's office. Despite this
volatile antagonism, the strategy and attitude espoused by Nagata
steadily gained preeminence within the military establishment.
The abortive February 26 incident in 1936 conveniently marked
the end of direct action and the decisive ascendency of the pragmatic views of Nagata and his followers, notably Tōjō Hideki
(1884–1948).

The Control Faction of the military did not stand on as complex (or interesting) an ideological base as the Imperial Way Faction. It was unconcerned, for example, with political ideas, such
as Kita's concept of social justice or Tachibana's utopian communalism. It did not place great stock in religious zeal, as in seeking out a traditional "faith." An uncomplicated patriotic loyalty
to the Japanese nation sufficed, and the emperor was not viewed

17 Maruyama Masao, *Thought and Behavior in Modern Japan*, pp. 66–74
and 302–3. See also Tōyama Shigeki, Imai Seiichi, and Fujiwara Akira,
Shōwa shi (Tokyo: Iwanami shoten, 1959), pp. 119–30; Ishida Takeshi,
Kindai Nihon seiji kōzō no kenkyū (Tokyo: Miraisha, 1956), pp. 247–88; and
Takahashi, *Shōwa no gumbatsu*, pp. 173–216.

as a mystical or dynamic principle as Kita saw him. The Control Faction did perceive the extraordinary crisis into which the nation had fallen and believed the nation needed to be "saved." But it identified the primary enemy as being those in the "regions" into which Japan had expanded, that is, outside the country, as in the Soviet Union, and not sinister elites on the homefront. Its political objective, therefore, was "expulsion" of the West from Asia and not "liberation" of the people at home. For these reasons, while Kita, Tachibana, and other radical patriots schemed for a restorationist revolution to destroy the existing constitutional order and rebuild a new one, the men in the Control Faction carefully planned to manipulate the bureaucracy, the *zaibatsu*, and the parties.

Despite this seeming identification with the constitutional order, the Control Faction was actually no less radical than the Imperial Way Faction. Indeed, as most Japanese historians have agreed, its threat to the constitutional order was more severe since its activities appeared legal and certainly contrasted with the more visible tactic of revolutionary terror. Thus, to achieve its goal of total mobilization, it supported a wide-ranging reconstruction of the political system under the general aegis of the military. Beginning with legislation in 1937, the bureaucratic mobilization of the country, including the direct management of labor and capital resources, was mapped out by leaders of the Control Faction and its bureaucratic allies in a newly created planning board (*kikakuin*). Deeply contemptuous of the bourgeoisie and decrying the wastefulness of parliamentary politics, these leaders sought the "reconstruction" of existing relations of power. Relying on language in current use, such as "new structure" (*shintaisei*), "new party" (*shintō*), "imperial assistance" (*yokusan*), and, more generally, "restoration," the military strengthened its grip on the constitutional order, redefining the character of coalitions to accord with its strategic aim of total mobilization for the final war with the West.

It is important to mention that although the Control Faction rejected the strategy of the coup d'état in Tokyo, it welcomed the formulation of a "regional strategy" in Manchuria to transform that area, through military initiative, into a model of controlled economic and military power. Indeed the defiant seizure of Manchuria in 1931 bristled with this ideology. There in Manchuria, without interference from civilian politicians, it was believed a model system could be erected that would be sufficiently powerful to ward off the Soviet Union, thereby also ensuring the autonomy of the homeland and anchoring a new order for all of East Asia.

The complex political relationships among military and civilian factions prior to the Pacific War have been recounted elsewhere and need not be summarized here. It suffices from the vantage point of this chapter to observe that the Shōwa Restoration recalled some of the main themes of the earlier Meiji Restoration. A utilitarian and pragmatic position insisted that bureaucratic instruments should be manipulated and used in the light of the immediate strategic needs of the nation, a theme that went back to the discourse on national defense strategy in late Tokugawa times. There was also rebellious activism directed against the ruling political elites at home. The activists were violently suppressed and expelled from the center in both cases: Yoshida Shōin, the radical loyalists in Kyoto, and Saigō and his allies after the Meiji Restoration suffered this fate, as did the activists in the Imperial Way Faction, including its ideologues Kita Ikki and Nishida Zei. Yet in both instances, violent action left an indelible mark on politics, throwing political relations into a state of confusion and thereby altering them. Both Ōkubo and General Nagata were victims of assassination for their bureaucratic insensitivity; yet in both situations it was the pragmatic "bureaucrats" who gained the upper hand in power relations and in directing the course of the restoration.

The historian is reminded, however, that revolutionary events such as the Meiji Restoration cannot be "restored" and repeated in historical time. They are "complete" unto themselves. It was not the Meiji Restoration that was incomplete, but the second attempt that was tragically abortive, bringing social justice neither to the Japanese at home nor Asians abroad. The revolutionary and transformational impulse that might have been embedded in Shōwa restorationism was in the end dissipated in the expansive "dream to liberate Asia" (*Ajia kaihō no yume*). As a regional strategy, Manchuria was a far cry from Chōshū, Satsuma, or Mito, semiautonomous territorial fiefs from which a defiant position might be taken against the center. Manchuria was pointed outward against opposition movements in China and mechanized Soviet power. And finally, while Ōkubo was a bureaucrat, he was one in the sense of the Tokugawa *samurai*-administrator, not in the sense of the technically trained military strategist in the manner of General Nagata in the twentieth century. With the passage of time, the restorationist formula for revolt and action had been rendered unworkable.

6

Epilogue:
Japan beyond Restoration

Although the Shōwa Restoration was abortive, it is well to be
aware of its radical character. However else one wishes to describe
restorationism in the 1930s, its underlying intent, clearly, was to
"reconstruct" the legal constitutional order or to challenge its
constraints with defiant actions, as in the streets of Tokyo or in
the distant region of Manchuria. This reconstructionist challenge,
moreover, came from men within the military establishment whose
loyalty to the nation and to its cultural spirit was unassailable. Its
net effect was to loosen previous bonds of political coalition, align-
ment, and compromise that had held together constitutional politics as a governing force in the previous eras of late Meiji and
Taishō and allow men to rise to political prominence who, under
a more firmly led and and stable context, would have remained
in the background.

Indeed, those called upon to provide constitutional leadership
were decidely less able than men such as Hara or Hamaguchi. The
aged genrō, Saionji Kimmochi, whose interest in politics was by
choice ambivalent, sought to give guidance from within the inner
reaches of the system by forming well-balanced coalitions. In the

end, however, he approved the appointment as prime minister in 1939 of Hiranuma Kiichirō (1867–1952), for whom he had little respect or liking. A stout conservative, Hiranuma had built a career in the justice ministry struggling against the expansion of parties in the Diet. Now Hiranuma came to pose as the defender of the entire constitutional system, including party and parliamentary politics, and supported Konoe Fumimaro (1891–1945) in curbing the excessive demands of the military. For assuming this posture, which contradicted his previous support for nationalistic causes, Hiranuma in 1940 was shot and gravely wounded by an ultrarightist and removed from the political arena. Konoe, as prime minister between 1937 and 1939 and again between 1940 and 1941, was an indecisive leader. Although viewed as an ideal leader by many at the time because of his aristocratic birth and his intellectual support of popular nationalist ideals, Konoe wavered ambiguously between "reconstructionism," the language used among advocates of the Shōwa Restoration, and defense of the constitutional system. Whatever may have been their other virtues, these men were not political leaders of the first order, and their rise to prominence in the pragmatic arena of coalition politics in Japan of the 1930s is far less suggestive of their actual political acumen as of the declining sense of certainty within the constitutional leadership and its inability, in the context of the turbulence of the 1930s, to adjust and reaffirm itself in terms of previous coalitions of power.[1]

The most striking evidence of this uncertainty was the rude treatment of Minobe Tatsukichi in 1935.[2] Verbally abused (and then physically attacked) for his view of the emperor as an "instrument" of the constitutional order, Minobe surrendered his seat in the house of peers. In contrast to the 1910s, there was hardly a rallying of voices on his behalf from within the very leadership in the constitutional order to which his ideas and scholarship had

[1] See Oka Yoshitake's paperback, *Konoe Fumimaro* (Tokyo: Iwanami shoten, 1972); also Itō Takashi, "Kyokoku itchi naikaku ki no seikai saihensei mondai," pp. 56–130.

[2] Miller, *Minobe*, pp. 196–253.

given ideological support. In short, the catalogue of political arrangements that provided order to constitutional government had been thrown into a state of disarray; and there can be little doubt but that the sudden and dramatic impingement of restorationism accounted for this political uncertainty.

Viewed from the perspective just outlined, it would seem that the Shōwa Restoration was not a logical extension of the Meiji constitutional settlement as has often been suggested in Japanese and Western historical accounts, but one among several articulate internal reactions against that settlement that maintained the constitution had had a constraining effect on Japan's modern search for certain expected objectives. The advocates of restorationism strongly believed their goals would achieve a final and lasting national autonomy and integrity from the interference of Western power. These goals would also define a set of ideal social ends such as democratic justice for the Japanese, accomplishments expected of modernity. The Meiji constitutional order, and the Meiji oligarchs who first designed and operated it, were viewed as having imposed an ineffectual form of bureaucratic rule with corrupt parliamentary politics appended to it. The psychological underpinnings of Shōwa restorationism would thus appear closer to other twentieth-century modes of protest and resistance to the constitutional order than as a mere extension of that system itself.

The problem of restorationism in twentieth-century Japan lies in a broader introspection about a history that failed the Meiji Restoration. Whether this view was conceptualized in the language and theory of popular nationalism, popular democracy, socialism, or restorationism, there was the common belief that the central vision of the Meiji Restoration remained unfulfilled and, indeed, that it had been betrayed at various critical points by bureaucratic leaders and that, furthermore, this betrayal had been given structural expression in the constitutional settlement of 1889. Needless to say, the intellectual justifications for criticism and protest were widely disparate: Yoshino Sakuzō's critical liberalism stressed the view that morally conscious and humane men could transform personal and social values and, in turn, the quality of institutions; Kawakami Hajime emphasized that the political order had been absolutized through a feudal monarchy and that, therefore, the entire system had to be swept away and rebuilt anew; Kita Ikki saw the opportunity to seize the popular monarchical symbol and use it for just social ends. While these intellectual perspectives are generic, pointing to the highly plural character of Japanese thought, it is of some significance to observe their common focus on the failure of the constitutional system to realize the goals believed proper to modern Japan. It is also worthy to note that there is a common concern with the quality and content of personal commitment, of finding a principled basis upon which to protest, and act out moral convictions.

What was being challenged, clearly, was not the egalitarian principle used as one of the organizing concepts in the constitution, a point underscored by Kita Ikki himself, but rather the expansion of bureaucratic power and an elitist ethos (*kanken bannō*) and the spawning of industrial and party politics within the constitutional order. Thus it was argued all along the spectrum of political criticism that while feudalism was destroyed through a restorationist revolt, it was replaced by a new inflexible structure, in its own way equally as arbitrary and despotic as the *bakufu* and dominated by new powerful and wealthy elites that used the egalitarian and popular vision of the Meiji Restoration for their own narrow, special interests.

It was this recognition of a modern authoritarian "superstructure" that decisively fed into the criticism, which became marked in the twentieth century, that constitutional reason, in theory and process, was not adequate for modern existence; and that there was a pressing need for a restoration or a reconceptualization of commitment to loyal action either through a theoretically more powerful conceptual construct such as liberalism or Marxism or through a more satisfying faith such as Ōyōmei idealism, the Buddhist ideal of "selfless love," or a mystical identification with the Lotus Sutra. This quest for intellectual "faith" in industrial Japan during the decades preceding the Pacific War suggests a deeply felt need for disengagement from politics as a necessary condition for critical personal commitment and is not simply an apolitical retreat into privitism as Maruyama Masao and others have tended to suggest.[3] It also suggests to us that the search for faith is a profound and often creative current in modern Japan, not a casual resurfacing of tradition.

It was militant restorationism, however, that meshed with modern Japanese culture, being solidly grounded in historical experience and having clear antecedents in modes of thought and of personalities. In the final analysis, therefore, the challenge that prewar politics poses to postwar Japan is how might this country achieve or develop toward the ideal image of itself as a just and creative social order without that radical restorationism as a persuasive historical model to fall back on, for it cannot be denied that the 1930s marked the last vigorous and sustained expression of restorationism in the modernization of Japan.

As a watershed in modern Japanese history, then, the Pacific War severely discredited the radical thrust of the Shōwa Restoration. It did not dissolve "feudalism" or "tradition" in the diffuse meaning of these terms. Loyal commitment to ethical and aesthetic ideals and service to persons and efforts greater than the particular self remained values central to Japanese culture and shall undoubtedly continue to be so. In our account we have emphasized the point of view that the legacy of Japanese feudalism is more than the idealization of harmony and loyal docility, a theme too often emphasized in the West. Japanese feudalism also included a strong ethical and emotional insistence on the validity of criticism and, on occasion, heroic resistance to history and arrangements of power. It was this activist tradition, especially as espoused by loyalists in the 1860s and military men in the 1930s, that received a crippling blow in the war and the ignominious defeat.

[3] Maruyama Masao's stimulating essay is "Patterns of Individuation and the Case of Japan: A Conceptual Scheme," in Jansen, ed., *Changing Japanese Attitudes toward Modernization*, pp. 489–531.

In a recording played on August 15, 1945, the emperor in a frail and high-pitched voice informed the Japanese people of the decision to surrender without condition. For centuries scholars and nationalistic pundits had said the emperor, as a god-king, represented something distinctive about Japanese culture, reinforceing, through cloistered and inactive elegance, the Japanese belief in the capacity of men to transform themselves into something other than what they are through extraordinary and creative effort. This charismatic image was irrevocably punctured in that moment of defeat. It is true that in assuming collective responsibility for the entire nation, the emperor helped to reduce the anguish of individual citizens. But clearly the emperor had been stripped of his divine spirit and placed beyond the reach of ideological manipulation. Under these unprecedented circumstances, the question facing postwar Japan was what its essential make up as a modern nation should be.

Although not immediately apparent, the answer to this question became clearly evident in the 1950s: The central and defining character of postwar Japan would be the sustained bureaucratic drive for reindustrialization. Recalling the first industrial revolution in the Meiji era, the postwar political and industrial leadership could not perceive a place for Japan on the international scene without the support of a powerful industrial complex. As in early Meiji, in such figures as Ōkubo Toshimichi, Kido Kōin, and Itō Hirobumi, there was a deep conviction that "wealth" always precedes "power." In a real sense, Japan did not have a "choice" about its reindustrialization, despite the early occupation plan to prevent it. The nation's educational experience, technological expertise, bureaucratic and managerial skills, and the steady and inexorable trend toward urbanization, all pointed to the resurgence of a technologically complex, industrial society. Ever since it launched itself onto a course of industrialism with the Meiji Restoration some one hundred years ago, Japan had irrevocably severed itself from the agrarian isolationism of the Tokugawa period and chose expansive industrialization, which not even the Pacific War, however ruinous, could reverse. Japan's industrial epoch, in short, began well before the Pacific War and was now being powerfully reinforced even as the country appeared hopelessly shattered by the war.

The political leadership in postwar Japan is clear about its identity with modern Japanese history. Obviously wishing to avoid a repetition of the 1930s, especially in regard to the lack of a strong constitutional leadership, it sees itself as the bearer of a pragmatic tradition that grew out of the Meiji Restoration and came to be woven into the constitutional settlement and the industrial transformation of the country. Central to this pragmatic legacy is the vision of Japan as a maritime and industrial nation, managed by a bureaucratic elite screened, tested, and proven as "men of talent."

As I have emphasized in this account, the intellectual foundations of this tradition are deeply rooted in the bureaucratic experience of the Tokugawa period well before the confrontation with Western power. During this period, bureaucratic behavior regularly repeated over time came to be viewed as a normative value identical with loyal action itself. The examples of Yamazaki Ansai and Ogyū Sorai in chapter 2 are suggestive of this tendency. These men sought to provide, although from divergent points of view, consistent theories explaining the validity of bureaucratic structures and of loyal and effective performance within them. Both affirmed the inevitability of bureaucratic hierarchy in society and also provided language for the discussion of political failure. In rational bureaucratic thought, the possibility of miraculous intervention in political process came to be viewed as unlikely, reinforcing the emphasis on pragmatic efficiency, functional specialization, and the reliance on fixed legal regulations.

The Meiji era that followed saw the rearticulation of the principles of bureaucratic utility, the inevitability of hierarchy, the desirability of normative constructs, all to allow a new and broader range to loyal service. It was intended that the search for constitutional certitude would result in a more consistent and less arbitrary structure of loyalty, contrastive to the system of *bakufu* rule in both design and performance. Although today's political leadership still refers back (especially in moments of informal candor) to the Tokugawa ideal of ethical bureaucratic performance, it is primarily to this Meiji view of "constitution" that it traces itself.

This idea that constitutional government means the rational and systematic exercise of bureaucratic reason was evident in Itō Hirobumi and became central to the thought of Minobe Tatsukichi. Whereas "reason" in Tokugawa times, whether defined as carefully formulated law or as ethical norm, pointed to the establishment of a structured "order," in Minobe it came to mean the rational exercise of constitutional intelligence to achieve ends that had yet to be realized. This is an ideology that prizes the structured exercise of "reason" over the identification with abstract principles, a fact that neutralizes the theoretical differences between the Meiji constitution and the MacArthur constitution. In whatever manner "sovereignty" is defined, in short, the constitution shall be made to operate according to the bureaucracy's perception of itself. It is a perception that believes bureaucratic leadership will surmount any obstacle to lead the nation forward. It is an elitism relatively free of corruption and filled with self-confidence.

This concept of "constitution" and "reason," however, did not mesh with a good deal of critical thinking throughout Japan's modern history. Beginning in the Tokugawa period a powerful countertradition developed that viewed with skepticism the ethical nature of bureaucratic hierarchy. The critique, as discussed in chapter 3, was couched in the language of philosophical idealism and of populist conceptions of the nation. There is here a utopian idealization of society as being without hierarchy so that the people (*bammin*) are one before the monarch (*ikkun*), whose thoughts, feelings, and values are identical with all of the people. All intermediary constructs, therefore, were denounced as false and obstructive.

This tradition of idealistic protest gained modern expression in the thought and movement for popular rights, popular nationalism, and liberal democracy. Emphasized in particular was the view that the central objective of the Meiji Restoration was the establishment of a new egalitarian order, as promised in the Oath of 1868, to unite the high and the low, that would include free public discussion and popular participation in national politics. The profound gap between the practical and instrumentalist perspective on constitutional government and the idealistic and populist expectations of it was greatly exacerbated in the twentieth century with the expansion of bureaucratic and industrial organization and the rise of partisan parliamentary politics. Needless to say, a similar gap persists down into the present.

In postwar Japan as in the 1920s, there continues an undertone of disquiet about pragmatic constitutional politics. The political changes that ought to have occurred as a result of the defeat in the war, it is pointed out, have not been extensive enough and reform has been reduced to mechanical distributions of wealth and power among narrow interest elites and has not been focused on the real human needs of society. The ineffectualness of the leadership is also criticized, as in its failure to establish a viable independent foreign policy. As before the war, the voices of criticism reflect divergent points of view along a broad and plural spectrum. Needless to say, the memory of the "failure" of constitutionalism before the war weighs heavily on the minds behind movements of criticism and protest. The convenient argument that democracy failed before the war because of structural defects of the Meiji constitution becomes less tenable as time goes on. As before the war, many still believe that democracy even under the new constitution exists in "name" only, not in "content." [4] While Western observers may point to Japan as a functioning democratic system, Japanese intellectuals and critics tend to view their political reality in a substantially different light, since for them the ethical principles in modernity and democracy are goals that have yet to be achieved.

It was out of this general sense of the failure of postwar politics that the celebrated novelist Mishima Yukio presented his

---

[4] See Matsumoto's introductory editorial essay in *Journal of Social and Political Ideas in Japan* 4, no. 2 (August 1966): 2–19; and Tsurumi Shunsuke, ed., *Kataritsugu sengōshi* (Tokyo: Shiso no kagaku sha, 1969).

passionate plea for the revival of traditional radicalism.[5] Referring back to the rebel Ōshio Heihachirō (see chapter 3), Mishima reminded the Japanese of the vital spirit of revolutionary commitment and protest that is intrinsic to the Japanese cultural personality. It is a commitment, he went on, that is uncompromising despite the certainty of defeat and therefore is ultimately symbolic and prophetic rather than strategic; it is, in short, a commitment to defy rational hierarchy and identify oneself totally to a just cause or, for that matter, a principle of beauty. Despite Mishima's heroic and sacrificial suicide (November 25, 1970) to dramatize his point of view, there has not been, and it is doubtful that there will be, a sustained resurgence of the radicalism that he idealized. His denunciation of economism certainly touched sympathetic chords throughout the country. But his emotional identification with the young radical officers of the 1930s marks him in the eyes of the Japanese public as an anachronism rather than a harbinger of a new political movement.

Western observers often suggest that critical opposition in Japan, whether of the "left" or of the "right" is made up of losers, men who never take power. This view misunderstands the character of protest in Japan. If one views modern society exclusively in terms of who gains power, then such a perspective may be defended. The view presented in this book, however, has been somewhat different. Political process in Japan has undergone drastic changes since the late Tokugawa period, and, in this history, political leadership has not reduplicated itself with predictive ease, as suggested in the shifts from *bakufu* bureaucrats to Meiji oligarchs to party politicians and military strategists. These shifts, moreover, have been accompanied by a continuous tension. It is worth remembering that bureaucrats such as Ōkubo, Hara, and Hamaguchi have fallen victim to radical attack, while on the other hand Ōshio, Yoshida, Saigō, and Kita have been destroyed by the established legal order.

Rather than view modern Japan in terms of winners and los-

---

[5] Mishima Yukio, "Kakumei no tetsugaku to shite no Yōmeigaku," *Shokun* (September 1970): 22–45.

ers, therefore, it is perhaps more revealing to see it in the context of an extreme interplay between the bureaucratic values which Ōkubo has been made to typify and the idealistic ones of Saigō. Between these archetypical modes is to be found in gradations and in a complex mix the dynamic reality of much of the Japanese cultural personality, the stuff out of which intellectual allegiances are made and unmade. Japan appears ambiguous to Western eyes in part because this intense interplay is often beyond their immediate purview and perception. The Japanese are of course profoundly aware of this dilemma in their culture. It is a deep and elemental dilemma that is central to modern Japanese history.

The future holds for Japan the continued refashioning of these extremes in imaginative and dynamic ways that will avoid the pitfalls of the past. This does not mean searching for an "identity," which implies the Japanese suffer from lack of one. It means rather working out a relationship between *conflicting* identities. Having reestablished industrial power with unprecedented skill and dedication, Japan faces an enormous task of persuasion, of gaining and maintaining the allegiance of its politically conscious and articulate strata, which are as extensive and complex as in any Western nation. The challenge is enormous, especially viewed through the perspective of the 1910s and 1920s, the so-called Taishō era, when such an allegiance could not be gained. It is a task that will have to be faced with much imagination and enlightened thought. On the other hand, the politics of protest also faces an enormous challenge. An awareness that the present course of history must be altered is matched by a recognition of the awesome power of the bureaucratic and industrial establishment. Clearly the periodic reliance on direct action, as in laying waste the universities in the late 1960s, will not lead to fundamental change. Beyond restorationism and the clandestine adventurism of the left there is need for a cogent and sustained strategy of protest. Seen in the light of the past, this too shall have to be confronted with imagination and intelligence. It is specifically in finding solutions to these modern problems that Japan searches for an identity.

Index

089217